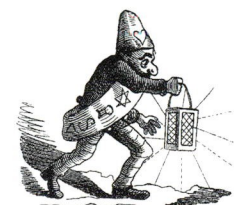

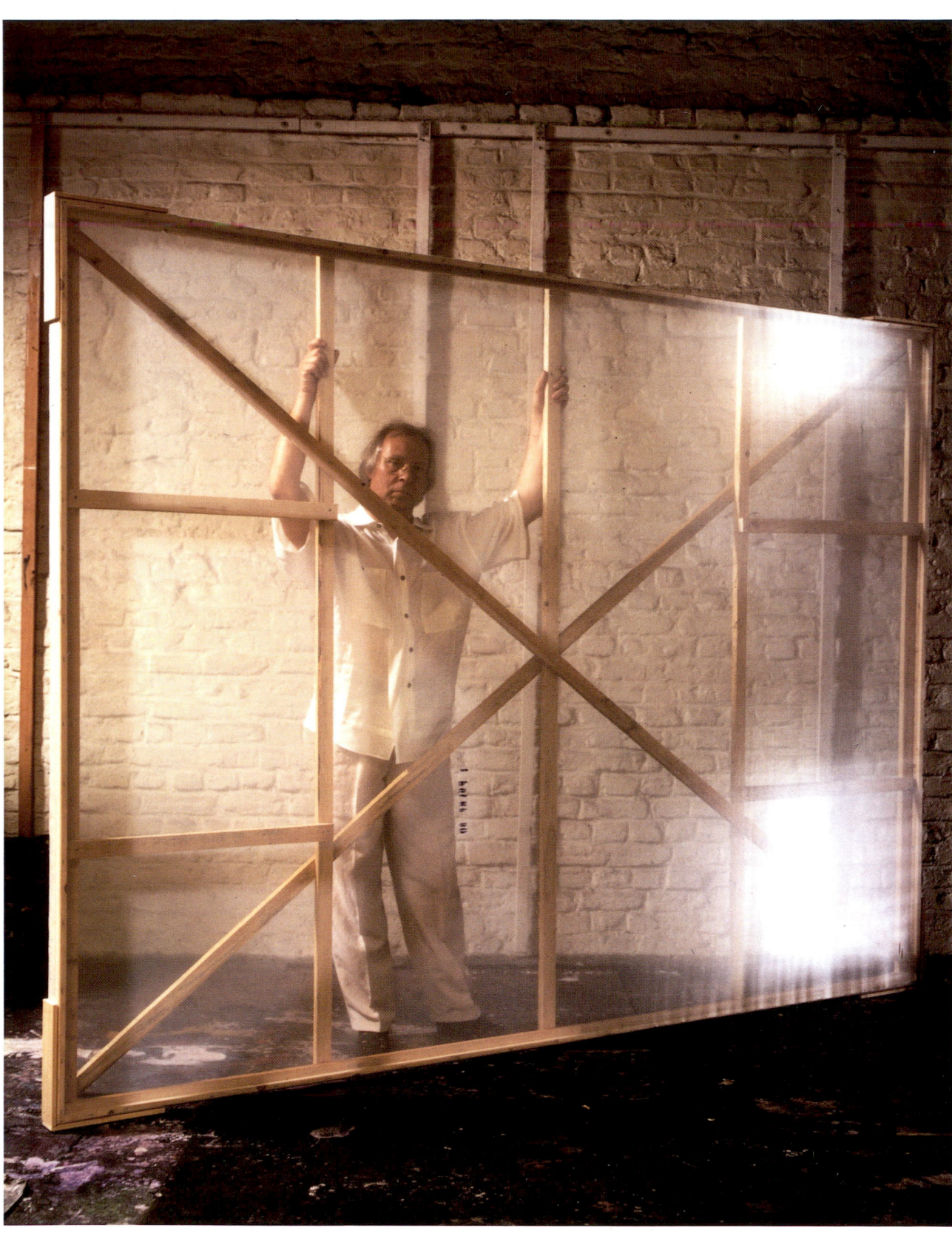

Sigmar **Polke**

Join the dots

TATE GALLERY LIVERPOOL

Contents

List of lenders

Private Collection, Courtesy Thomas Ammann Fine Art, Zürich
Block Collection, Denmark
Collection Froehlich, Stuttgart
Collection Garnatz
IVAM. Instituto Valenciano de Arte Moderno – Generalitat Valenciana
Private Collection, London
Helen van der Meij
Georg Polke
MNAM Centre Georges Pompidou, Paris
Raschdorf Collection, Düsseldorf
Collection Speck, Cologne
and several private collections

Preface

Sigmar Polke is widely acknowledged as one of the most significant artists working today. His free-wheeling imagination has not waned over three decades, during which time he has confounded critics, amazed his fellow artists and delighted us all, as his work has crossed many borders around the world.

It is hard to believe, therefore, that this is the first survey of Polke's paintings to be seen in this country. His work was represented at Tate Gallery Liverpool in *Art from Köln* in 1989, whetting the appetite for a larger showing. The present exhibition provides an opportunity to see Polke's painting in all its variety, from the tongue-in-cheek humour of the Capitalist Realist works, through the increasing complexity of his painted surfaces and his startling inventiveness with materials, to the sheer beauty and shining wit of his recent work.

With such dexterity of mind and hand, Polke's works will continually subvert any attempt to trace a neat line of development. His career does not tread a line – but circles and twists like a doodle, and sometimes wanders right off the page.

This exhibition brings together over sixty paintings from public and private collections in Europe. It would be possible to present a very different kind of retrospective, one which concentrated on his photographic output, for example, but such is the unbounded nature of Polke's creativity, that one showing would never contain it. The exhibition was curated by Judith Nesbitt, Exhibitions Curator at Tate Gallery Liverpool, who selected the works in discussion with the artist.

We are indebted to the many owners of Sigmar Polke's paintings, whose generosity and enthusiastic support have made the exhibition possible. Our sincere thanks also go to Helen van der Meij, the artist's agent, who assisted us at every stage of the project, with characteristic good judgement. Sean Rainbird and Thomas McEvilley have contributed catalogue texts of originality and insight, for which we thank them.

We are, above all, indebted to the artist, whose acentricity and wit brought much merriment to the making of the show, suggesting that this work, while it is here, will be very much at home in Liverpool.

Nicholas Serota
Director, Tate Gallery

Lewis Biggs
Curator, Tate Gallery Liverpool

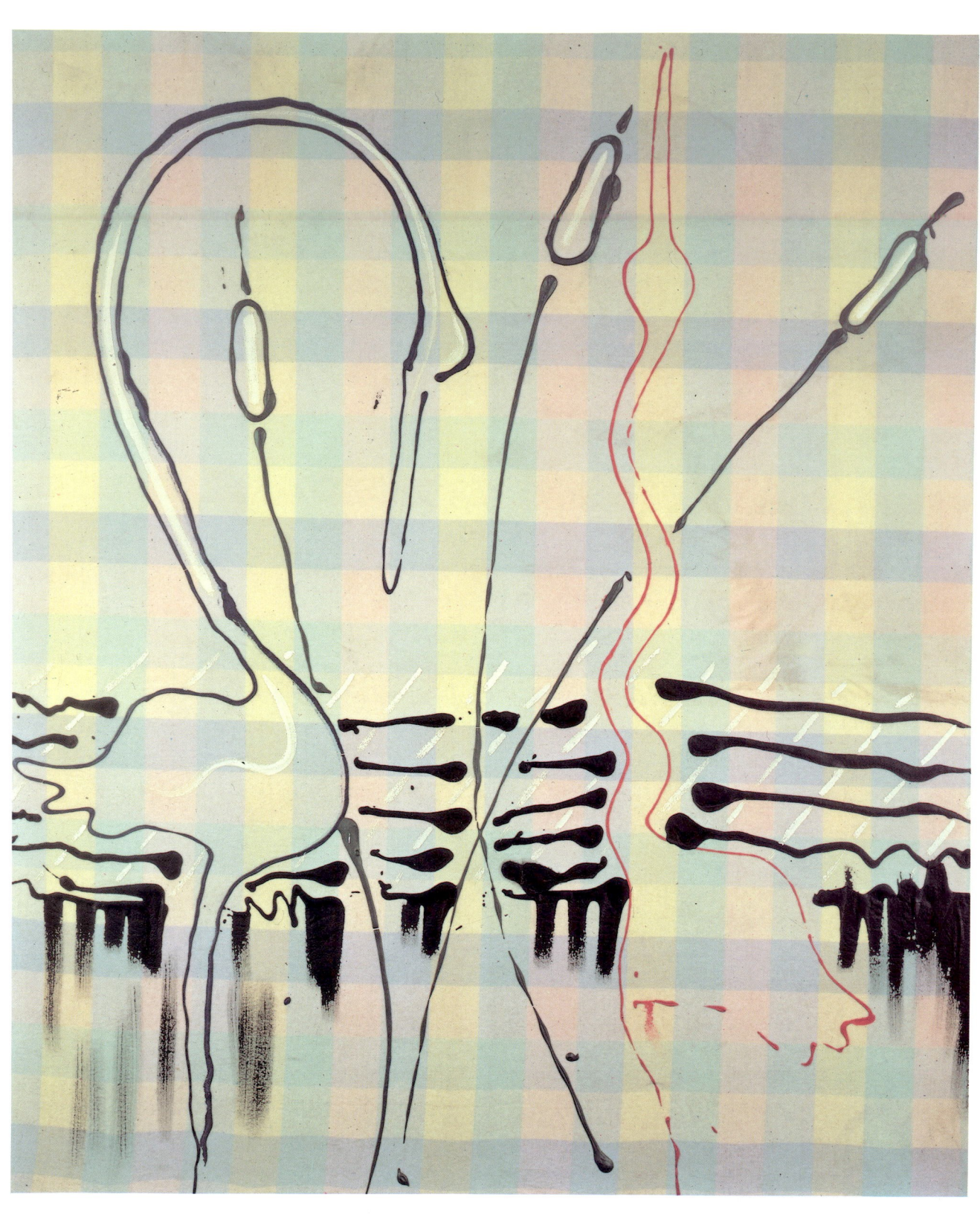

21. *Heron Painting II* 1968

Seams and Appearances:
learning to paint with Sigmar Polke

Sean Rainbird

Sigmar Polke is one of the most inventive artists working today, for whom conventions in painting exist to be challenged. This he invariably does in a wittily knowing fashion that acknowledges the historical relevance and parameters of those conventions, before extending them. Over the last three decades, Polke has investigated the power of images to communicate during a period when they appear ever more disposable because of their mass availability, the growing means for translating and transmitting them, and their increasing de-materialisation. While remaining essentially a figurative painter, Polke has extracted new meanings from paraphrased and borrowed images, through layering and juxtaposition. In this process other elements of the picture – its physical support structure, the materials used in making it and the way those materials are combined or applied – have been radically re-assessed. Polke examines the picture as a whole, in which its basic components are given equal status, rather than standing in hierarchical relation. Painting, far from being a redundant practice in an era of mechanical, electronic and digital communications, is shown by Polke to be a resourceful medium, equipped to investigate the complexities of contemporary experience.

Polke's art is as elusive as he is himself. He has constructed a persona that plays with the concepts of inspiration and originality. Within this cult of creativity, he is an elfin presence, a shrouded mystic, a magician projecting illusions (relishing the opportunity to execute his latest vanishing trick). He has also appeared as the alchemist, dabbling with the basic substances of the physical world. Polke projected himself in the 1960s as the agent whom Higher Powers directed to 'paint flamingos', 'paint the upper right-hand corner black' and conduct 'telepathic seances' with William Blake and Max Klinger, his artistic forbears from an earlier century. He constructed an eccentric etymology for his name, superimposing the letters of his name over a sketch of an Egyptian standing under a palm tree. In the accompanying text ('Sigmar Polke. Early influences, later Consequences or: How the Monkey Got Into My Business and Other Icono-biographical Questions'), published in 1976, he related the palm tree (a well developed theme in works of the 1960s) to 'Palmin' (a coconut fat; almost inevitably a reference to Joseph Beuys) and finally to Prometheus, the human who defied the gods and was punished for his impertinence. While suggesting his role as the agent of superior forces, Polke paradoxically asserted his absolute right to form and interpret the visible world in his own inimical manner – and accept the consequences.

During the 1960s, Polke was closely associated with the short-lived German variant of Pop art called 'Capitalist Realism' together with Gerhard Richter and Konrad Lueg (who stopped painting shortly afterwards). In October 1963, Lueg and Richter 'exhibited' in a Düsseldorf furniture store arranged as a modern sitting room, sitting in armchairs on pedestals as 'living sculptures' while their paintings hung in other departments. Their ironic transformation of the artist into a consumer object reflected the radically changing relationship between fine art and commercial culture.

Increasingly prominent in the 1960s were interdisciplinary activities such as performance art and Fluxus 'happenings' which combined dance, music and actions. Many artists were more concerned with participation than permanence, and multiple objects and prints were cheaply produced and widely distributed. Between the mid-1960s and early 1970s, Polke produced a body of prints (one a collaboration with Richter), as well as several unique objects, such as *Polke's Whip* 1968 (p40). He photographed a series of palm trees made with a variety of materials, such as balloons, a collapsible measuring stick, cotton wool, a glove, etc., for a print series published in 1966. He captured the trivial frustrations of making art in his *Boredom Loop* 1970, made of masking tape stuck to a studio wall. Polke's humorous one-liners were similar in their informality and modest scale to the objects in Fluxkits or multiples by Joseph Beuys, Blinky Palermo and many other artists. Beuys conceived of art as the engine for social and political change, rather than an activity confined within the walls of the art gallery or academy. His subversive presence on the staff at the Düsseldorf Academy, where Polke studied in the early 1960s, was in marked contrast to the formal instruction then given.

Karl Otto Götz and Gerhard Hoehme, who taught Polke at the Düsseldorf Academy, belonged to a generation of artists whose careers developed during the 1940s and 1950s, influenced by the twin centres of abstract art in Paris and New York. The introduction of mass-produced objects and photographic imagery in art of the late 1950s and 1960s made the art movements of tachism, art informel and post-painterly abstraction appear increasingly sterile and formalist, and cut off from the pace and character of everyday life. In Europe and America, Pop artists such as Richard Hamilton, Andy Warhol, Roy Lichtenstein and Polke, freely combined mass media imagery in their works, using serial structures to reflect the replication and instantaneity of mass production. They imitated the look of photo-mechanical reproduction, based on grids of minute dots of different density which, when magnified, gave the characteristic raster of Lichtenstein's enlarged cartoon stills or Hamilton's beach scenes. European Pop artists generally remained more attached

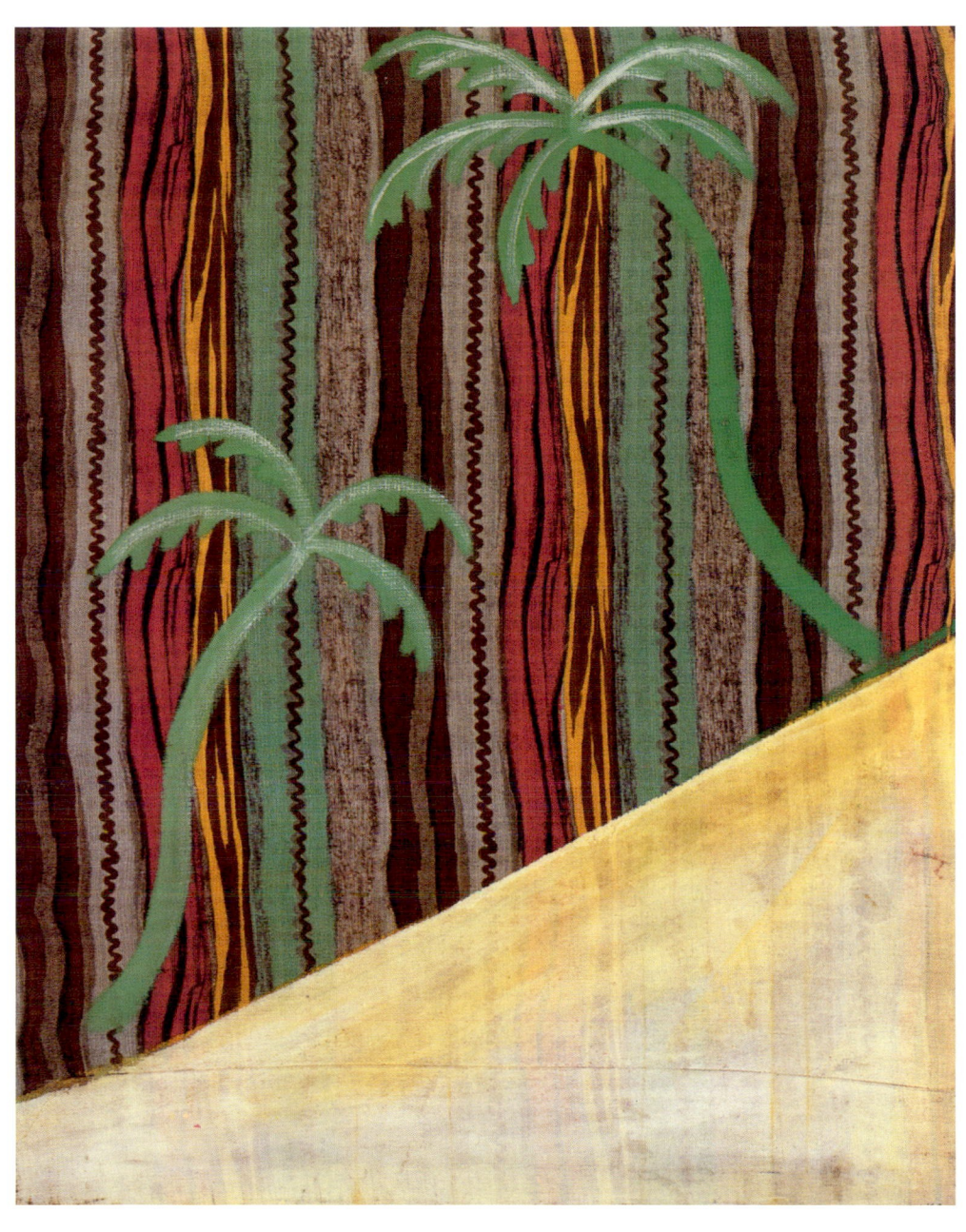

2. *Two Palm Trees* 1964

to the hand-painted surface than their American counterparts, who took the transfer process to its logical conclusion and silkscreened photographic images directly onto their canvases.

Polke's preoccupation with dots lay in a fascination with the devices and codes by which knowledge is structured and imparted. The magnified dots are based on a system of mechanical reproduction that denies the authentic touch and thus reduces the aura of individual 'finish'. This strategy is clearly visible, for instance, in the benday dots of Lichtenstein's paintings. Polke, however, negated the system's effectiveness by corrupting its simple codes. He magnified the dots beyond recognition, and in *Girlfriends* 1965, for example, he combined dots of a different scale and colour. On other occasions he corroded the system itself, so that the dots congealed and forfeited their function of carrying information. In these endless hand-painted variations and combinations lay, ironically, the power of the painter to undermine the dominance of the subject.

Warhol's 'do-it-yourself' paintings of the early 1960s such as *Do It Yourself: Sailing Boats* 1962, presented some of the most radical insights into the practice of painting. They proposed the redundancy of traditional concerns with composition and colour, and reduced the subject and craft to a banal exercise in painting by numbers. Warhol's provocative questioning about subjects for art and valid ways of representing them, was conducted using the subject of painting itself. They were closest in spirit to Polke's sensibility in their clever deconstruction of the practice and purpose of painting. Warhol indicated that the bargain bookstore was a more appropriate place to find an image than within the imaginative scope of fantasy and invention. However, as cultural objects they ultimately retreat from the conclusions they suggest. Warhol's 'factory' for images was predicated on the ruthless marketing of its originator as a celebrity.

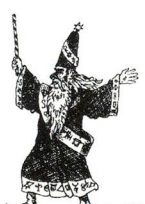

From the early 1960s to the present day, Polke has preferred to use commercially produced, often pre-printed fabrics instead of straightforward canvas supports. In so doing, he paradoxically gains a freedom to explore painting itself without being dominated by the iconic status of the subject. The fabrics he used suggested instead that even the painter's support belonged as much in the everyday world as in the studio. The idea of a blank surface awaiting the autograph mark is

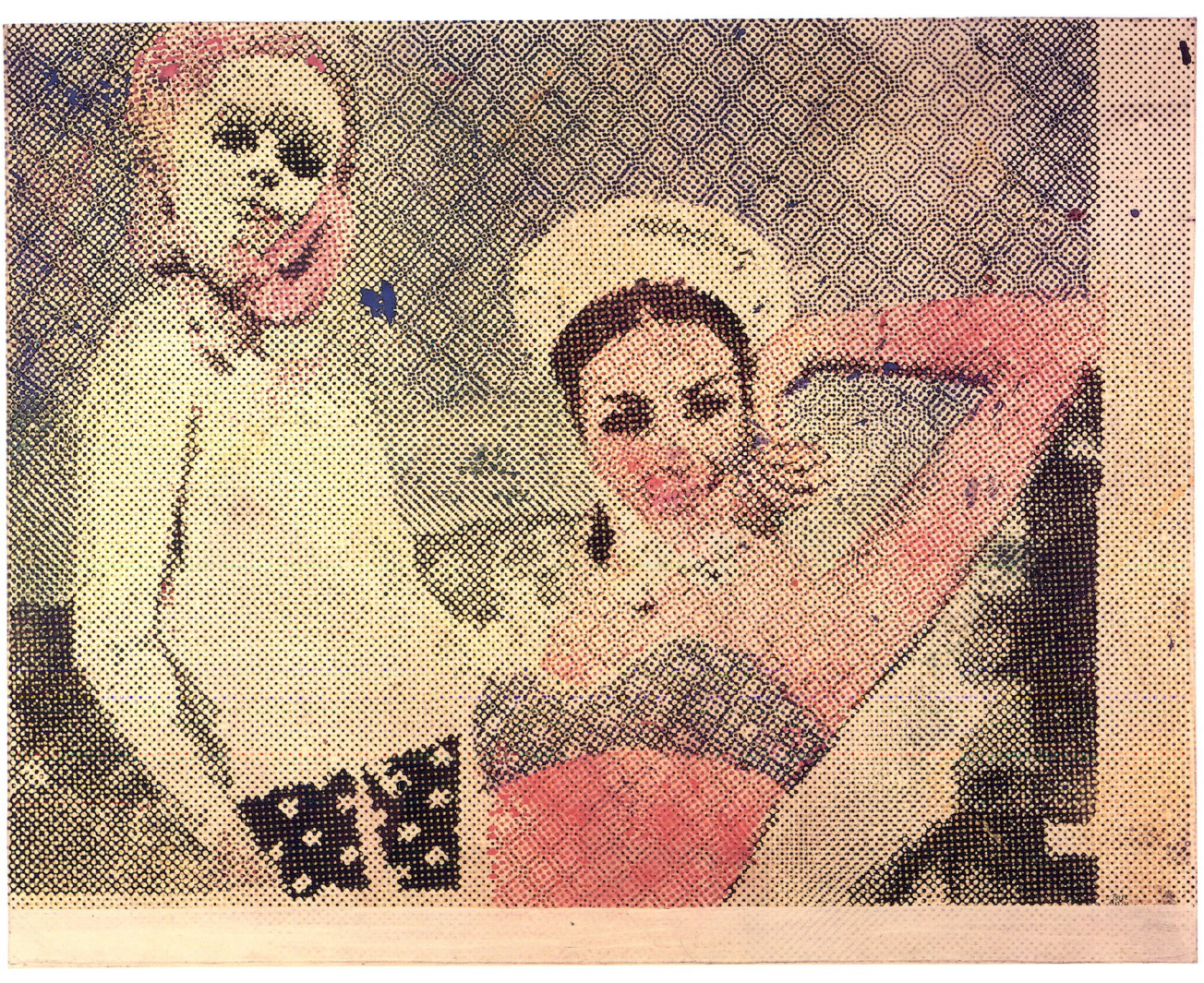

10. *Girlfriends* 1965

22. *Profile* 1968

made obsolete by the presence of pre-printed fabrics and finishes. Polke immediately establishes a relationship to something that existed before the picture, while simultaneously diverting that material from its intended function and transforming it into something unique. His *Profile* 1968, made by linking up the syncopated white stars of the patterned cloth to delineate a smiling profile, demonstrated just how minimal his intervention needed to be.

Moreover, by combining the handpainted with pre-existing designs (in a matter-of-fact acceptance that no image exists in isolation) Polke was free to exploit the effects of layering and disjunctions of scale. These are amply demonstrated in *Alice in Wonderland* 1971 (p45), or in the multiple narrative sources derived from Max Ernst and Goya in *This is how you sit correctly (after Goya)* 1982 (p67). With apparently endless diversity and the facility to combine disparate sources, Polke's paintings have remained supple and surprising.

Polke's art spoofs, such as his series of mathematically incorrect 'solutions', suggested that different sets of rules govern art and life. Their combination of text and image demonstrated that while words can describe pictures, only rarely can language and logic adequately explain them. Nonetheless, these paintings indicated the tenuousness of contemporary artistic practice, which could so easily be undermined or invalidated. Beneath the penetrating humour, Polke appeared to argue that painting was not a self-sufficient entity, but rather a discipline that needed illumination through other methods of enquiry. In most of Polke's visual gags, a detailed knowledge, or instinctual awareness appears behind the throwaway gesture. The tiles in *Carl Andre in Delft* 1968 (p36), for example, with their sailing boats and cardinal compass points, suggest the placid flatness that inspired the rigorously expansive horizontality of Andre's square, multi-unit floor sculptures.

It is the very crassness of Polke's images of the 1960s, derived from holiday brochures and glamour photographs such as *Woman at the Mirror* 1966 (p17), and their apparant ham-fistedness, that admitted the individual spirit in the handmade – for example, in the clumsy vertical brushstrokes in the 'stripes' series. By superimposing the lines of his hands over printed fabrics, or a world map, Polke asserted the ancient claim of artists to dominate the external world by visually colonising its territories and giving it an image of itself.

In the 1970s, it appeared almost as if the richness of possibilities in Polke's sewn textile supports and the cosmic complexity of finding a legitimate role for painting, stifled his images, which became clogged and incoherent, losing their mercurial freedom and fantasy. Polke's response was to suppress his role as originator or author through collaborations with artists such as Achim Duchow and, eventually to abandon painting for most of the decade. Instead, he turned to photography and its chemistry of exposure and development. He investigated film and video, frequently in collaboration with others. These activities grew out of the lifestyle he led at the time, which included experimentation with hallucinogenic drugs and casual, communal living.

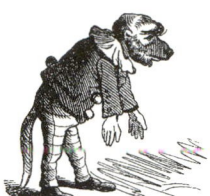

Polke's return to painting in the early 1980s was accompanied by a thorough re-examination of the content in his images, and by extraordinary resourcefulness in his use of materials. His subjects – often depicted in the form of elaborate allegories – became encoded commentaries on the conditions governing historical events, first in Germany's recent past, more recently, for example in *Children's Games* 1988 (p85), in the revolutionary epoch of late eighteenth century France. One of the earliest was *Paganini* 1981–3 (p18), in which Polke depicted the violin virtuoso and romantic composer on his deathbed, conducting a tune played by the devil perched on the side of his bed. On the left a juggling skeleton in clown's garb tosses a ring of skulls into the air, which land on the other hand, transformed into symbols of radioactivity. Breathtaking virtuosity and sublime creativity, Polke appears to argue, are unleashed as the devil's own tune, if they fall into the wrong hands. A swastika picked out in the pattern of the fabric recalls the spectre behind recent German history and the political dangers which cannot be mitigated by profound cultural achievements. *Camp* 1982, *Degenerate Art* 1983 and the *Watchtower* series painted midway through the same decade, addressed similar anxieties, while reactivating this long suppressed theme as a legitimate subject for painting.

Polke's careful search for a valid form of contemporary painting through an investigation of its recent history was most brilliantly achieved in his installation at the Venice Bienale in 1986. Framed by the German pavilion which was built during the Fascist era, Polke presented a spectacle that linked the ancient past of natural history (through the presence on the gallery floor of an iron meteor) with present-day images. A wall painting on the curving apse responded to changes in humidity during the course of the exhibition. Other paintings, made of resins or ground minerals, related the paintings to the basic elements of the universe. A series of eight paintings of florid curlicues decorating Dürer's woodcut of c1518 depicting the triumphal procession of Emperor Maximilian I, introduced the dimension of cultural history. As Laszlo Glozer explained, they symbolised the entrance of the artist, 'who interferes with the course of natural history so that he can teach us to be deeply moved consumers of beautiful pictures'.

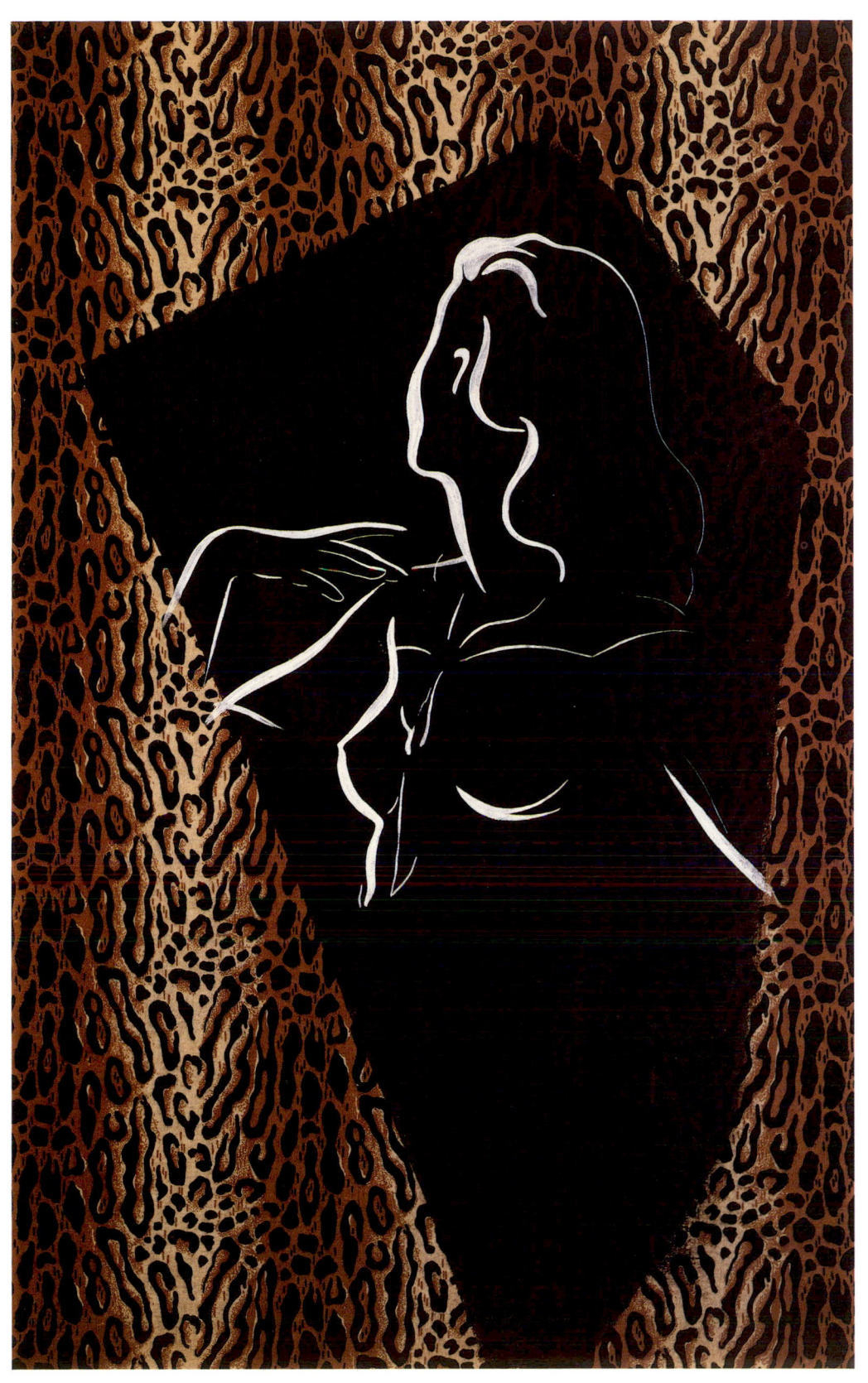

12. *Woman at the Mirror* 1966

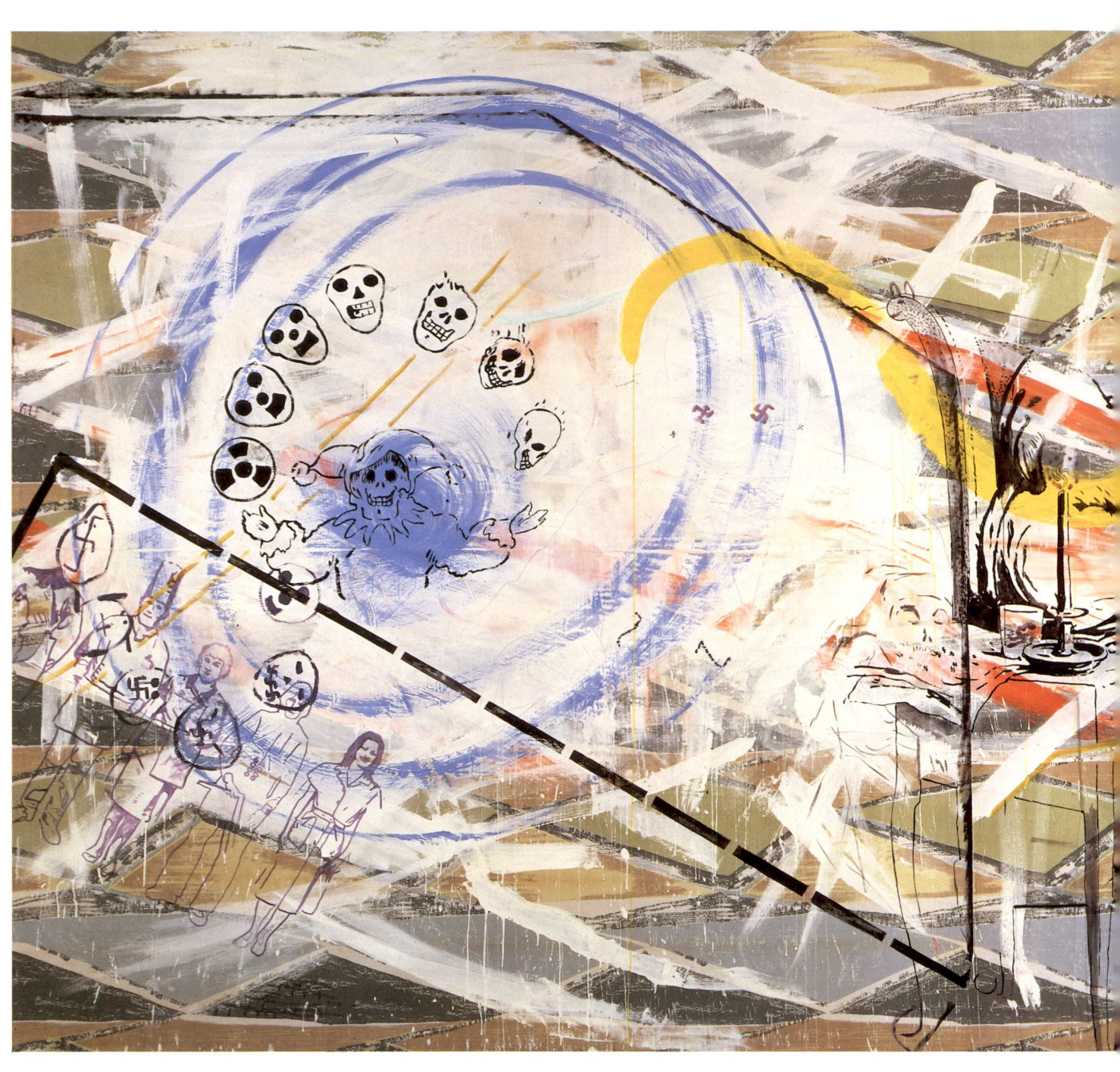

26. *Paganini* 1981–3

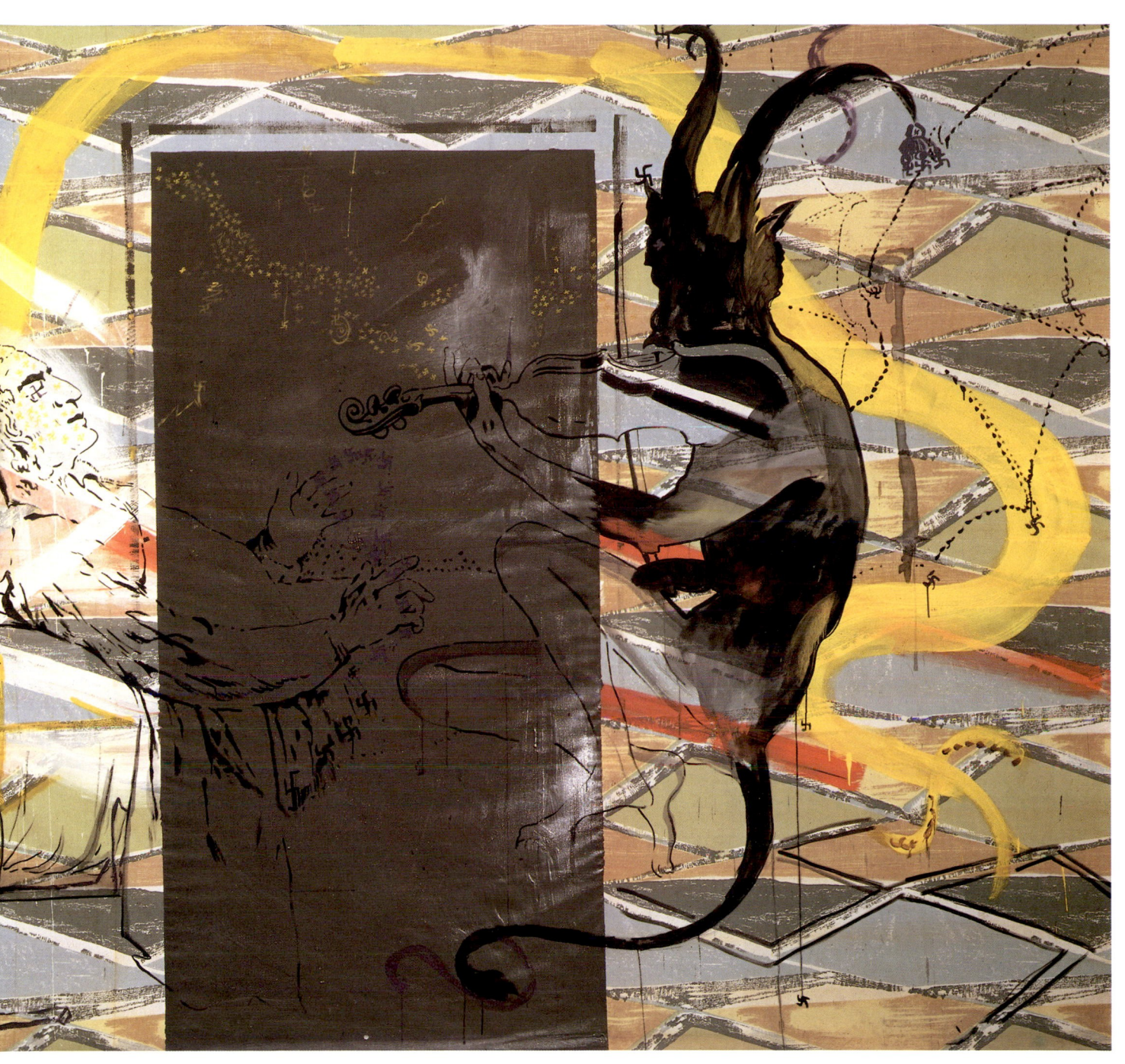

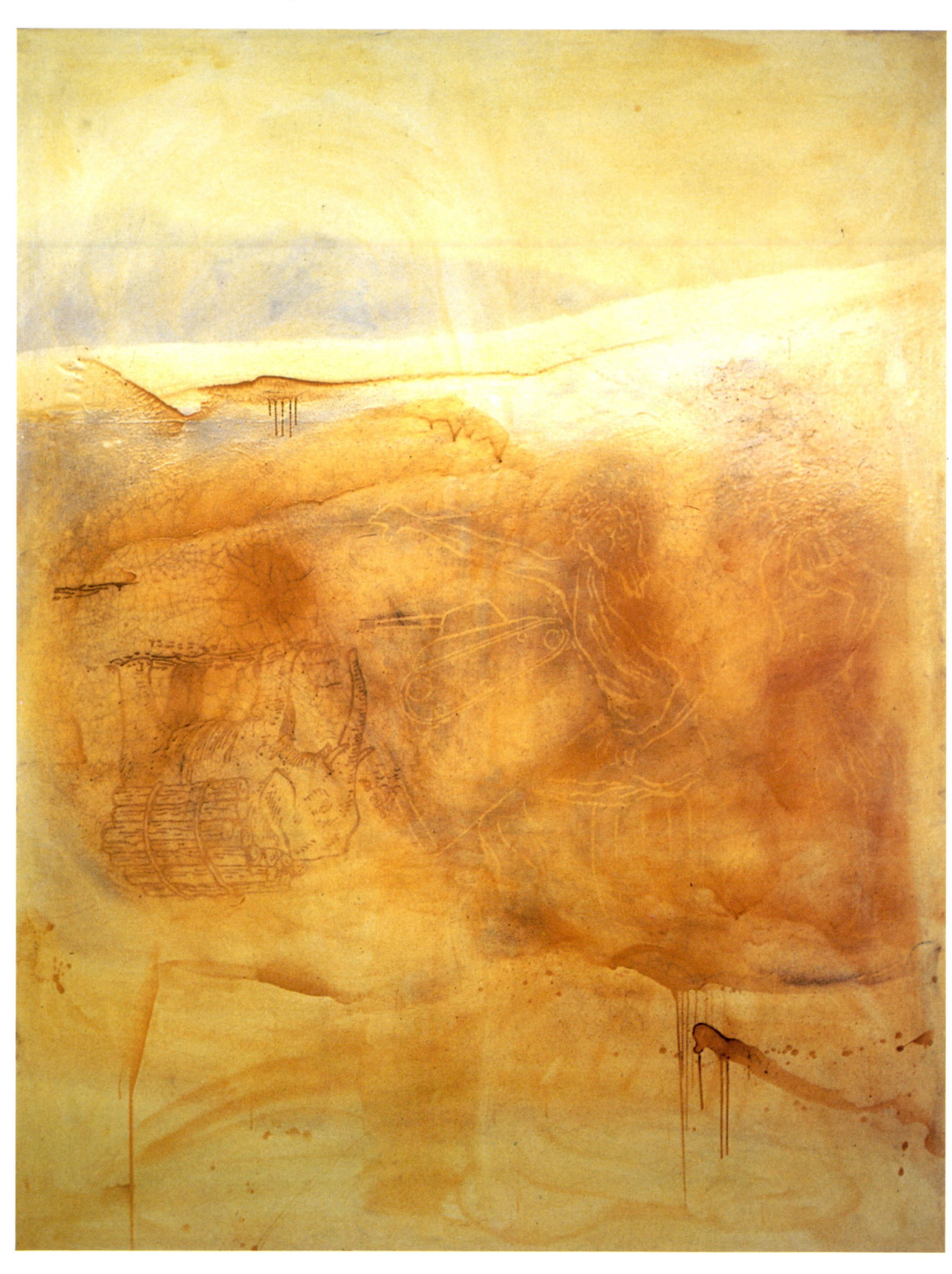

40. *Hannibal with his Armoured Elephants* 1982

Polke's thorough investigation of his materials and pigments in the 1980s marked further changes in his art. He began using a wide variety of substances and suspensions, and dramatically increased the dimensions of his paintings to accommodate their expansive flow. As in Venice, he created surfaces that reacted to changes in heat and humidity in what amounted to an alchemical investigation into the properties of colour and the mutability of the painter's materials. It is surely no accident that swiftly transforming natural phenomena, particularly cloud formations, recurred as subjects. Polke's concoctions blended the traditional skills of the pre-industrial artist's studio with the medieval apothecarist. He re-united, like Beuys, disciplines and knowledge systems that pre-dated a separation of art from science and regarded them as a single branch of learning. Polke's experimentation with hair-raising mixtures was pursued in the spirit of a search for profound knowledge, based on the essential elements of the physical world.

His application of gold leaf, hardened resins, or mineral compounds commandeered highly volatile physical forces that had a direct influence in the content of his paintings, while dramatically expanding the admissible colours and admixtures available as legitimate tools for the painter. Brilliant colours were frequently toxic, as with Schweinfurt green and orpiment (which contains arsenic). Substances that can kill have, in fact, long histories of medicinal usage in small dosages. The traditional risks of the painter – in using toxic white lead, for example – were translated by Polke from the materials into the content of the paintings themselves.

The malediction of *Radioactive Waste* 1992 (p22), is underscored by the dangerous compounds and admixtures Polke was using at the time, whose instability or toxicity look so harmless as a painted surface. The painting depicts a group of humans in protective suits picking over the ground with geiger counters. The image is barely readable through the congested raster of dots, printed over a patterned, reflective ground. Nuclear fallout is intangible, but its very invisibility and extreme corrosiveness stimulate extreme anxiety. Polke's image sets this preternatural fear against the elaborate procedures devised for measuring and containing radioactive waste.

Another visible development in Polke's art of the 1980s was his radical reinterpretation of the support structure in pictures. He re-defined the support not as something on which to project images (which predisposed it as something passive and opaque) but as something carrying the painting in its totality. More recent investigations have further undermined the hierarchical relations between subject, medium and support and realigned them as equal components in a picture. Many recent works can be read from either side because the images are painted, glued or sewn on translucent or reflective grounds. Images on the reverse can be seen from the front, disrupting and altering our physical perception of the image. The wooden

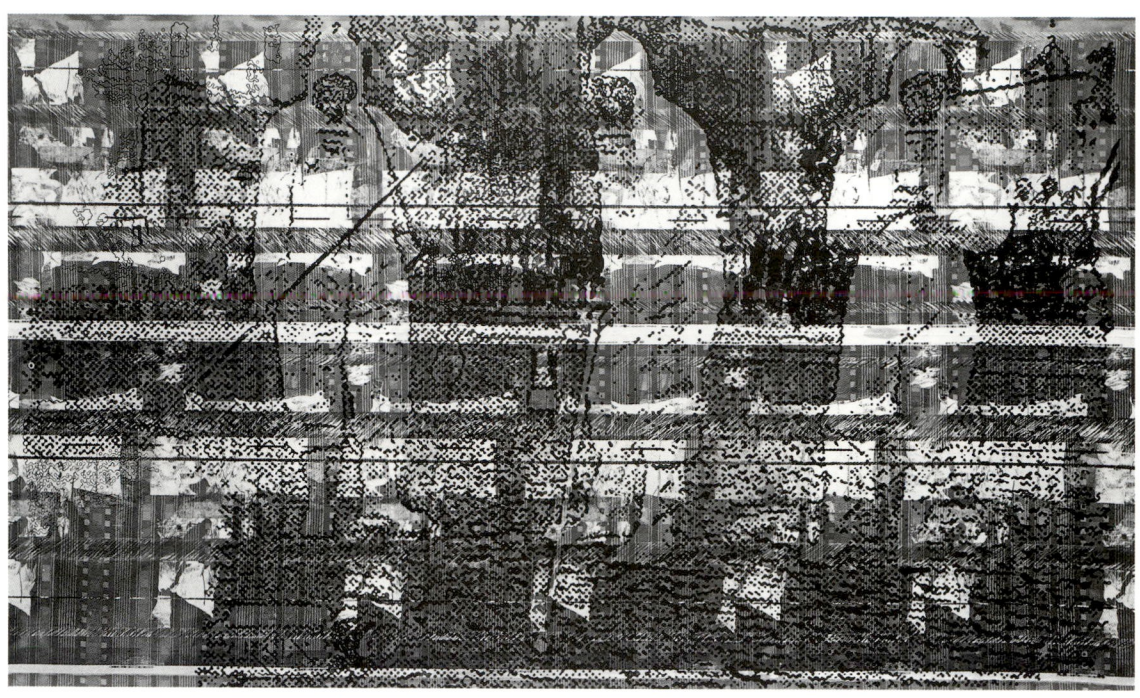

Radioactive Waste 1992, artificial resin and lacquer on fabric, Stedelijk Museum, Amsterdam

stretchers are rendered visible and enter the material structure of the image, reinforcing lines or divisions in the image itself, such as in *The Three Lies of Painting* 1994 (p99). In these works he exposes the flimsy assumptions of the conventional picture surface that reads as a projection from a point outside the picture. Light is activated as an ambient energy illuminating the totality of the picture. By painting on both sides, Polke confirms the image as something multifaceted, insubstantial and as acutely unstable as the materials he has used.

Polke appears now to delegate ever more processes in his painting, while remaining in ultimate control. His motifs are usually found within the history of art and illustration, or in theoretical treatises. They are often readable only as fragments depicting human agency, against the increasingly unstructured grounds on which he has limited the autograph mark by allowing the liquids he applies to find their own final shape. He has recently begun sewing in manufactured objects. One such painting is *Measuring Clothes* 1994 (p23), with men's shirts attached. The garments provide a form of visual shorthand to counterbalance the complex diagrammatic projections depicted in the line engravings elsewhere in the painting. Real objects are used to trump the visual devices whereby three-dimensional forms are traditionally depicted. By showing this so programmatically (at a time when he is

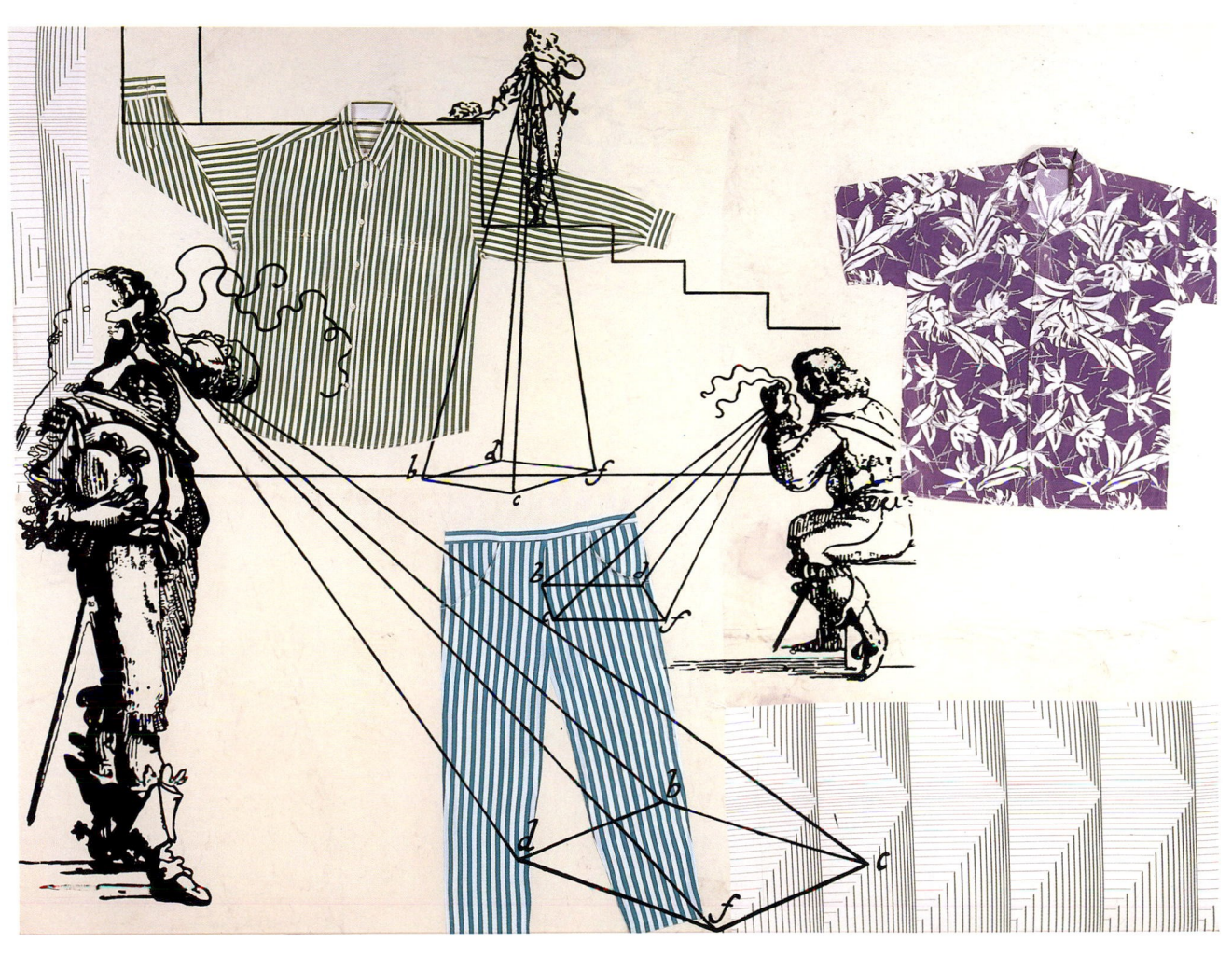

63. *Measuring Clothes* 1994

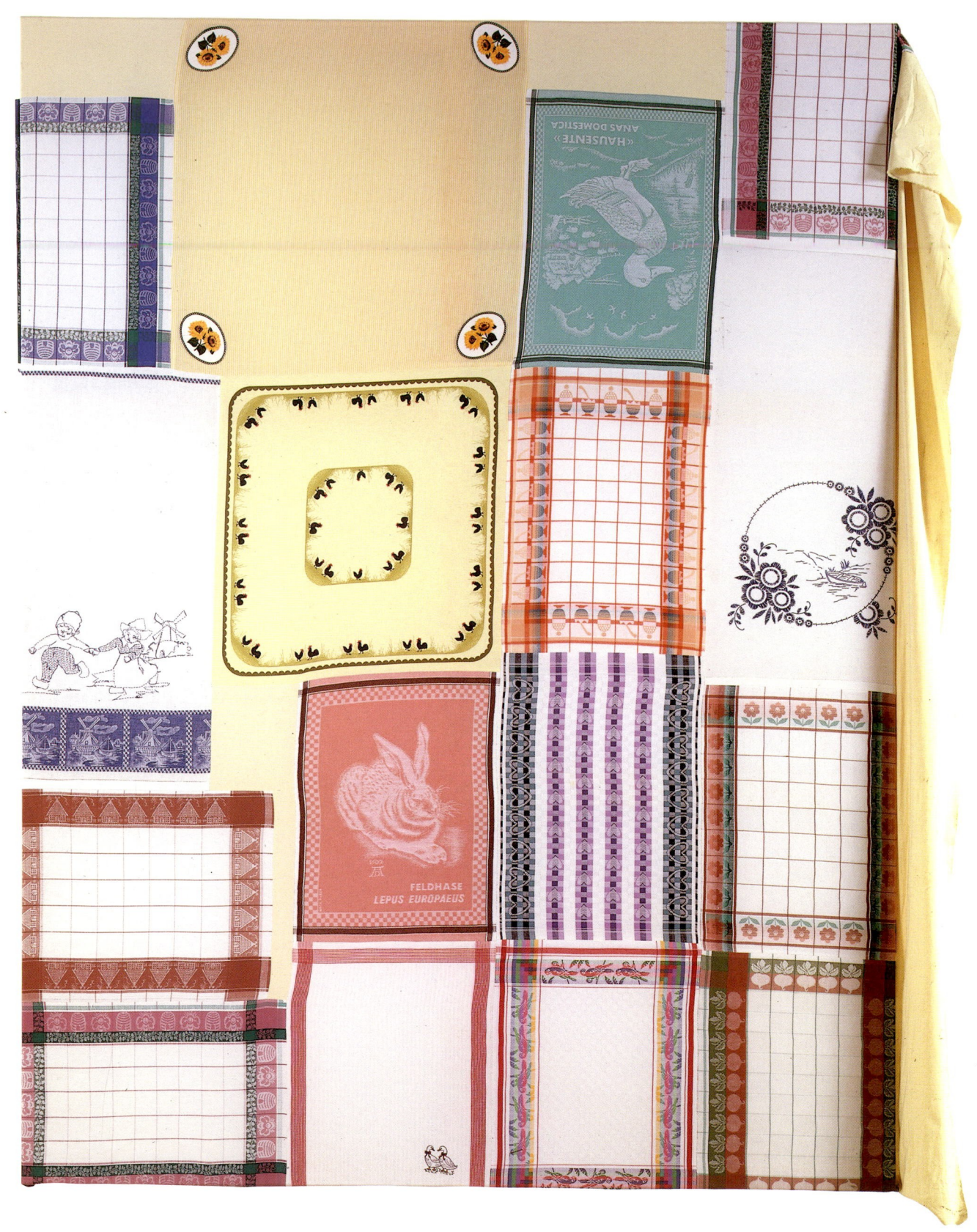

53. *Tea Towels* 1994

examining the physical substance of the painting) Polke reconfirms the continual exchange in his work, visible since the 1960s, between the painting as object and the painting as an image.

In *Tea Towels* 1994 (p24), Dürer's famous image of the hare, which first appeared in his work in the late sixties, is incorporated into a loose mosaic of washing-up cloths sewn onto a cotton backing fabric. Their designs and motifs provide a neat compendium of genres, a shortcut history of still-life, landscape, formalism, geometric abstraction, monochromy, collage and the ready-made in art. Dürer's original hare (for we cannot assign it to anybody else, even at this remove) is now only a distant relative, just as Polke's teasing work appears distanced from the conventional conception of a painting. Its context is, of course, the gallery not the kitchen, but *Tea Towels* characteristically contests any neat closure that decrees that the cloths could never revert to their original function. The right-hand edge of the canvas, hanging loose, lays bare Polke's conceit. *Tea Towels* embodies the physical and conceptual requirements for a picture and holds together the edifice by a thread. It is either an act of faith or a sleight of hand. Polke's paintings are nourished by a scepticism as to the continued efficacy of the medium and his desire to furnish it with the most convincing images his materials can support.

1. *Wardrobe* 1963

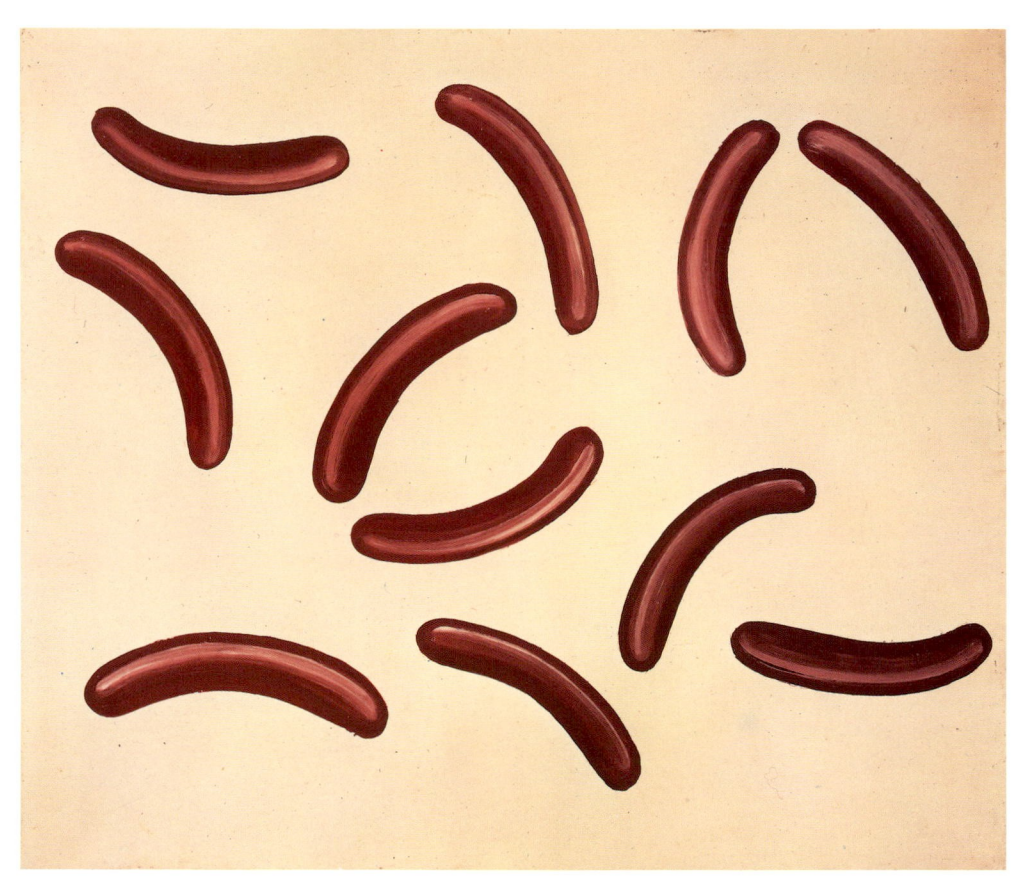

3. *Sausages* 1964

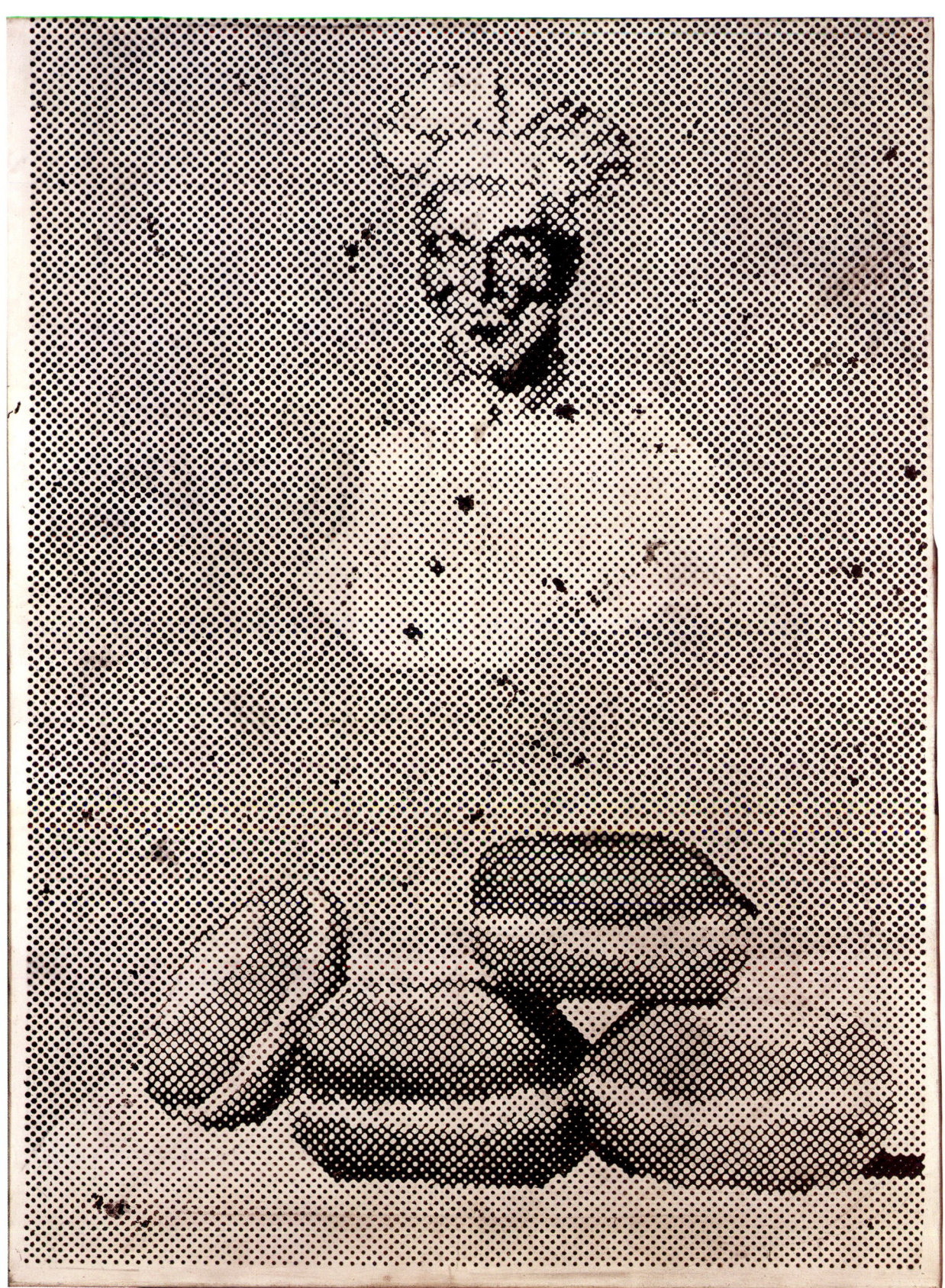

7. *Berliner* 1965

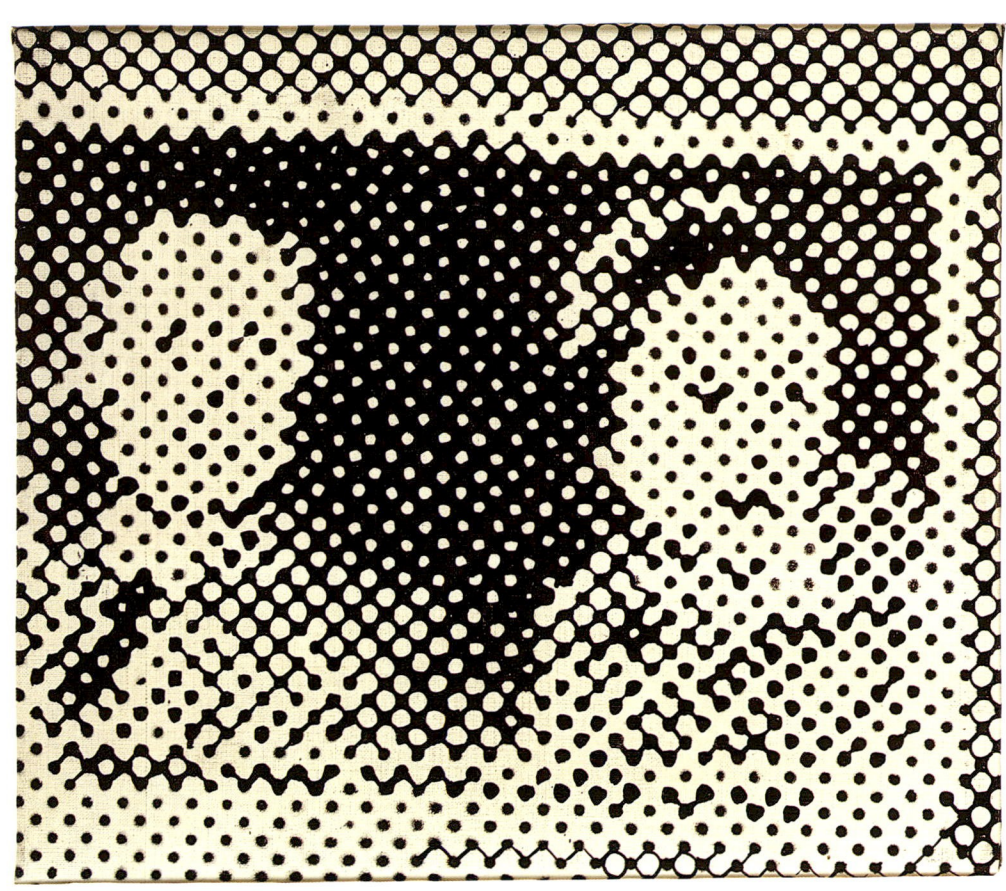

6. *The Duke and Duchess of Windsor* 1965

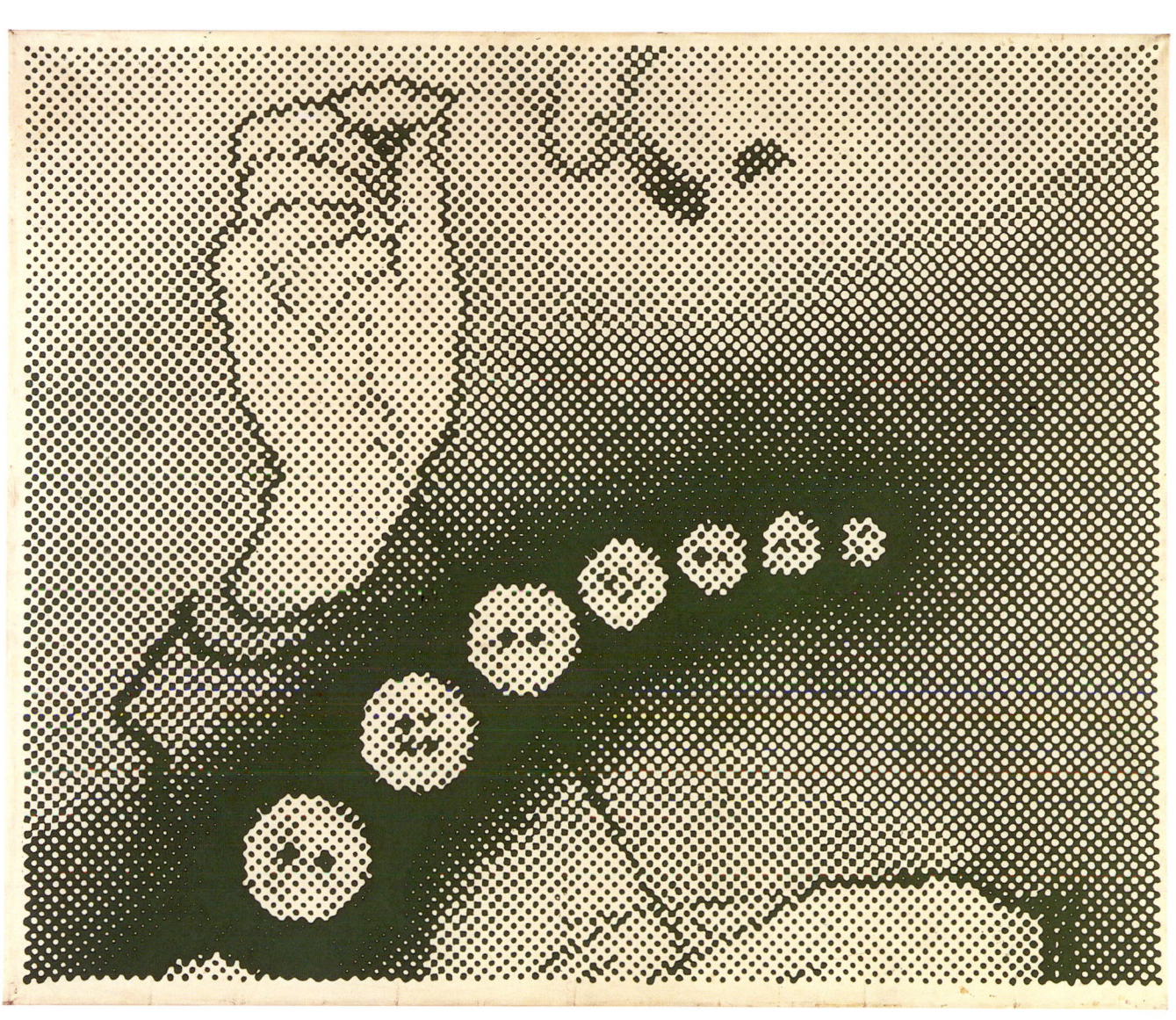

5. *Buttons* 1965

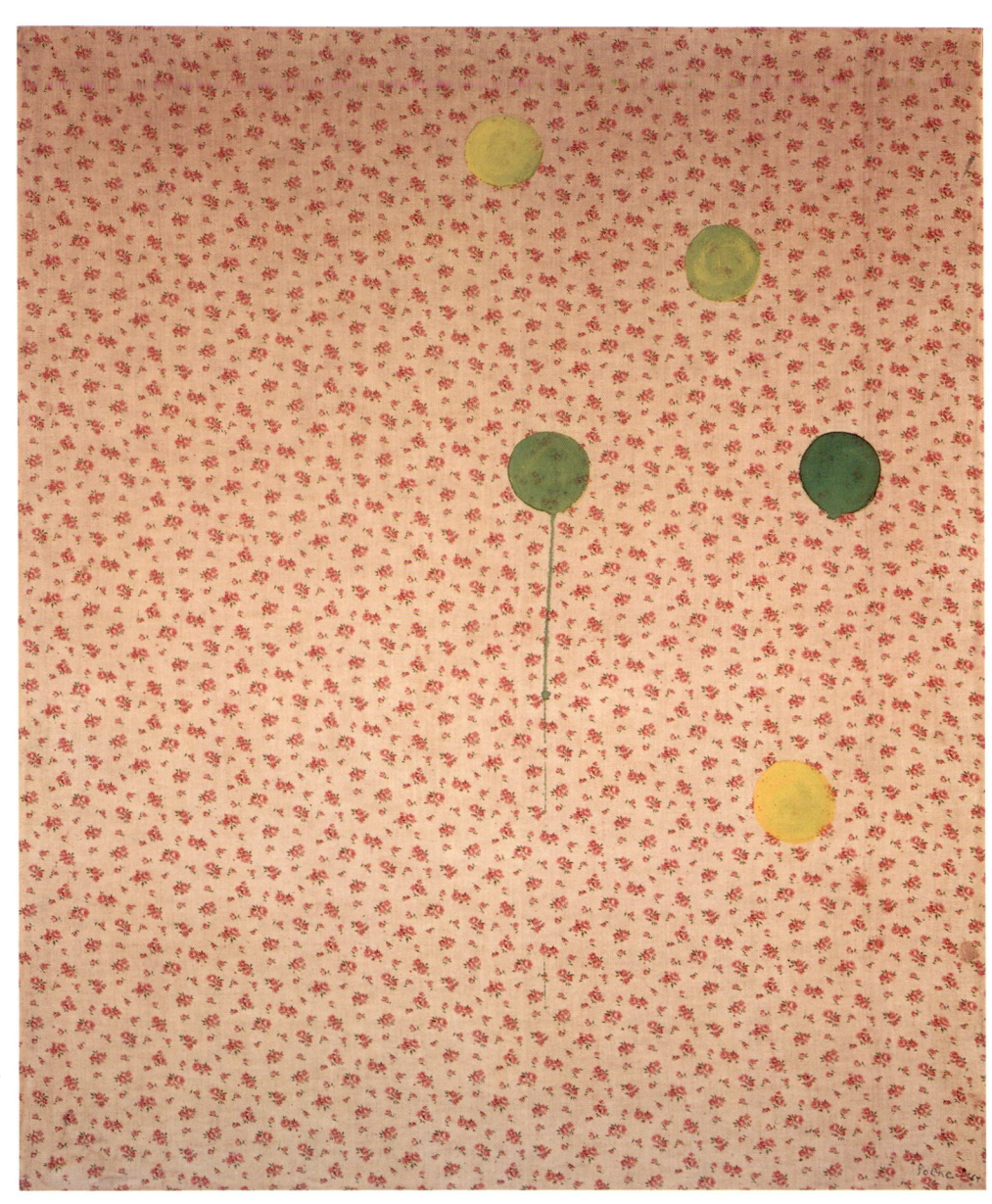

4. *5 Dots Painting* 1964

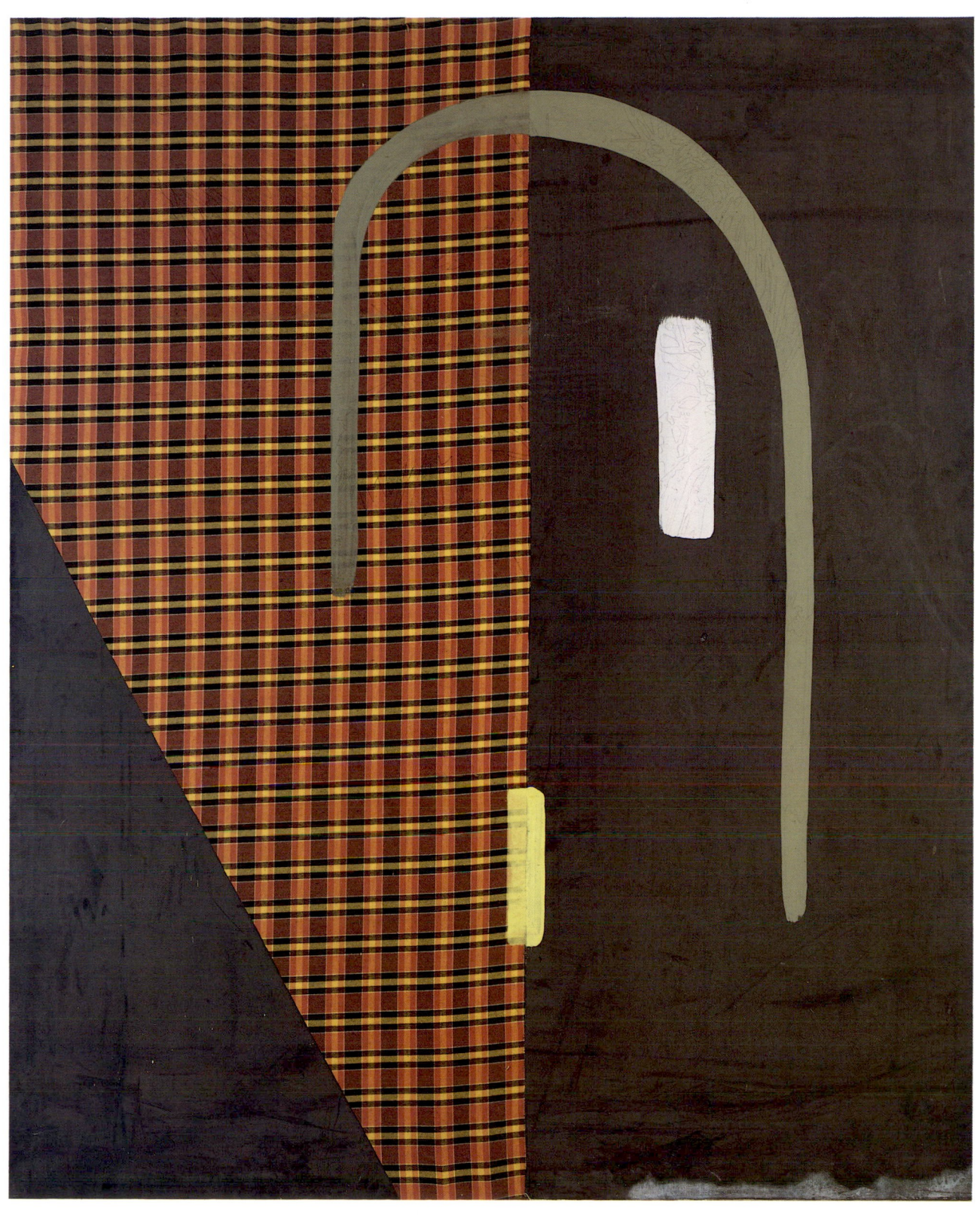

9. *Arch* 1965

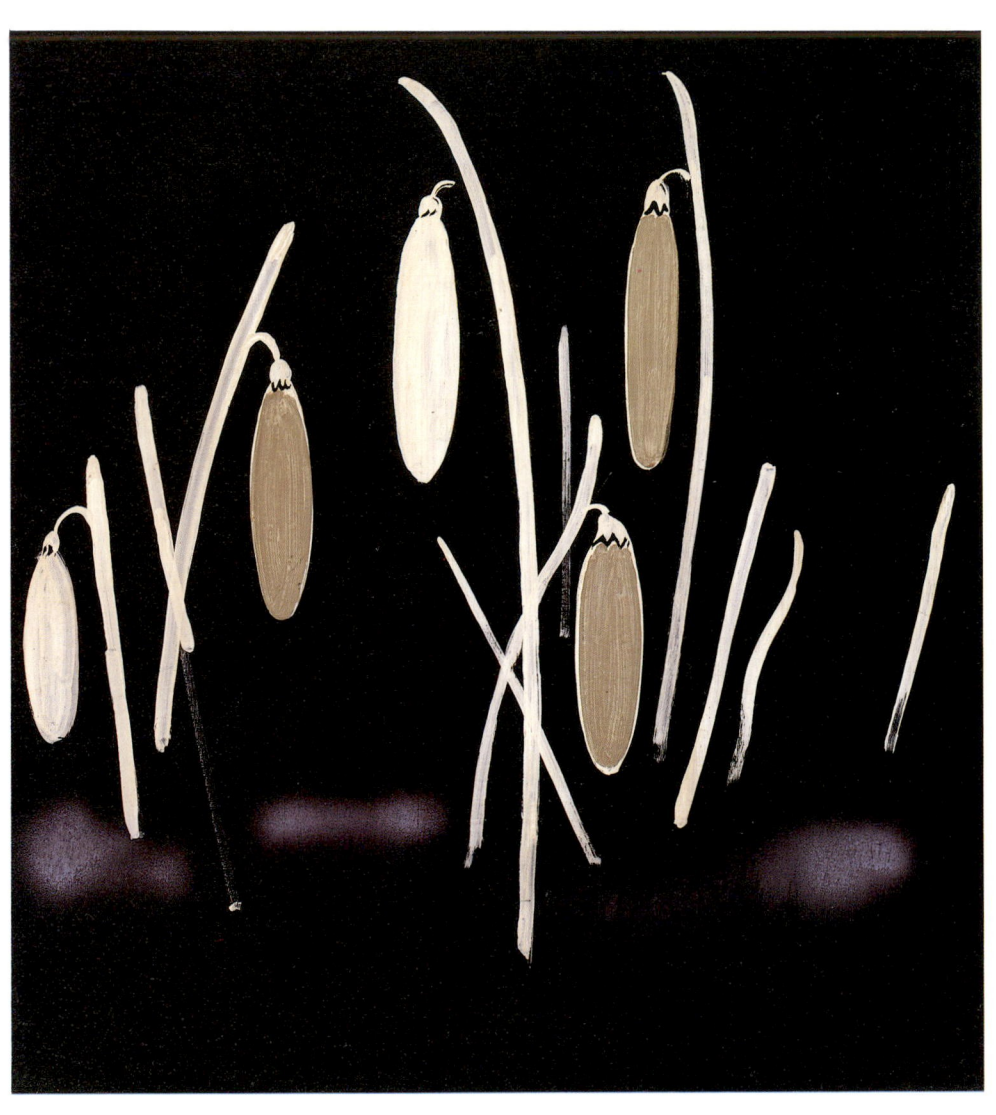

11. *Snowdrops* 1965

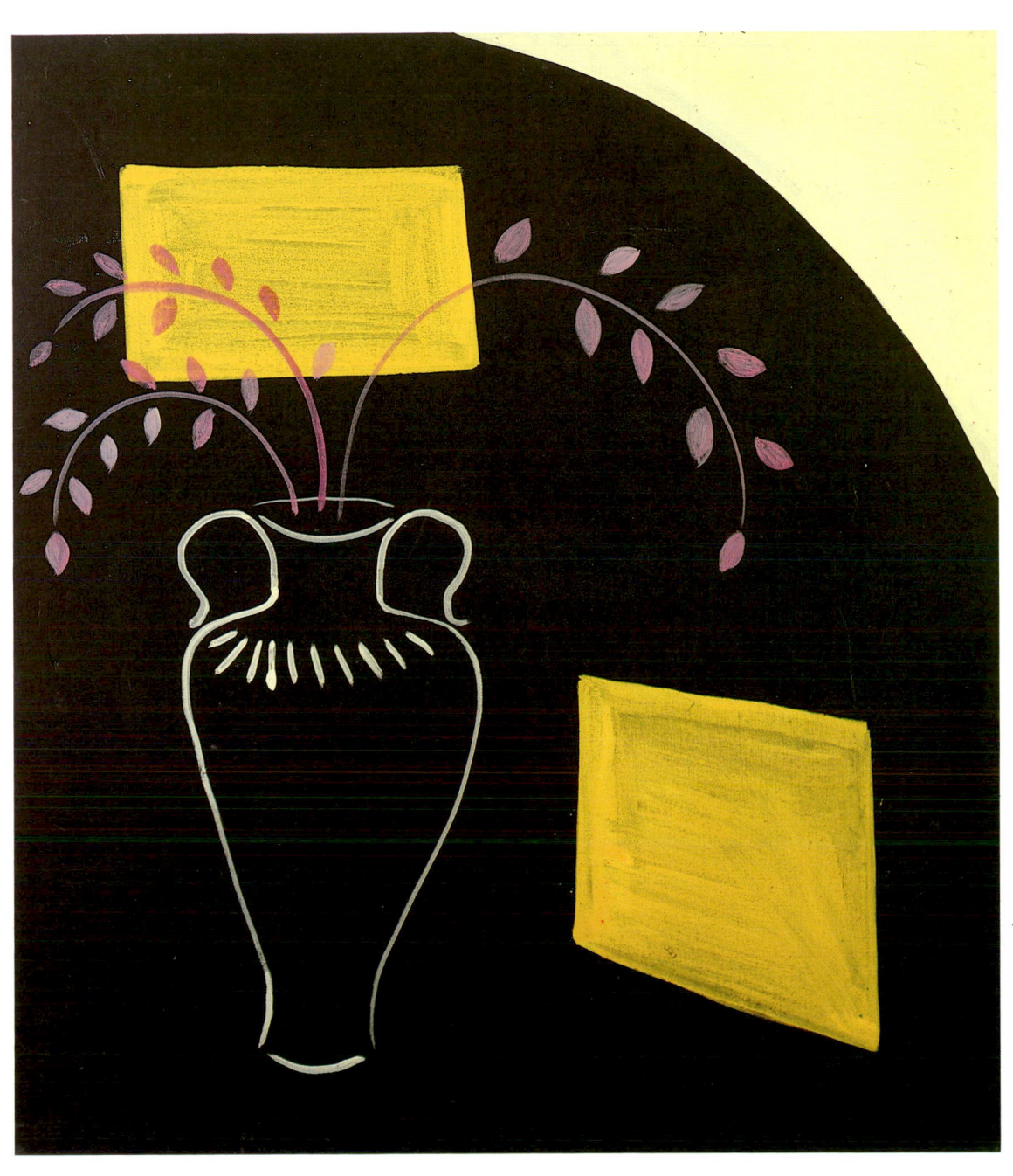

8. *Vase I* 1965

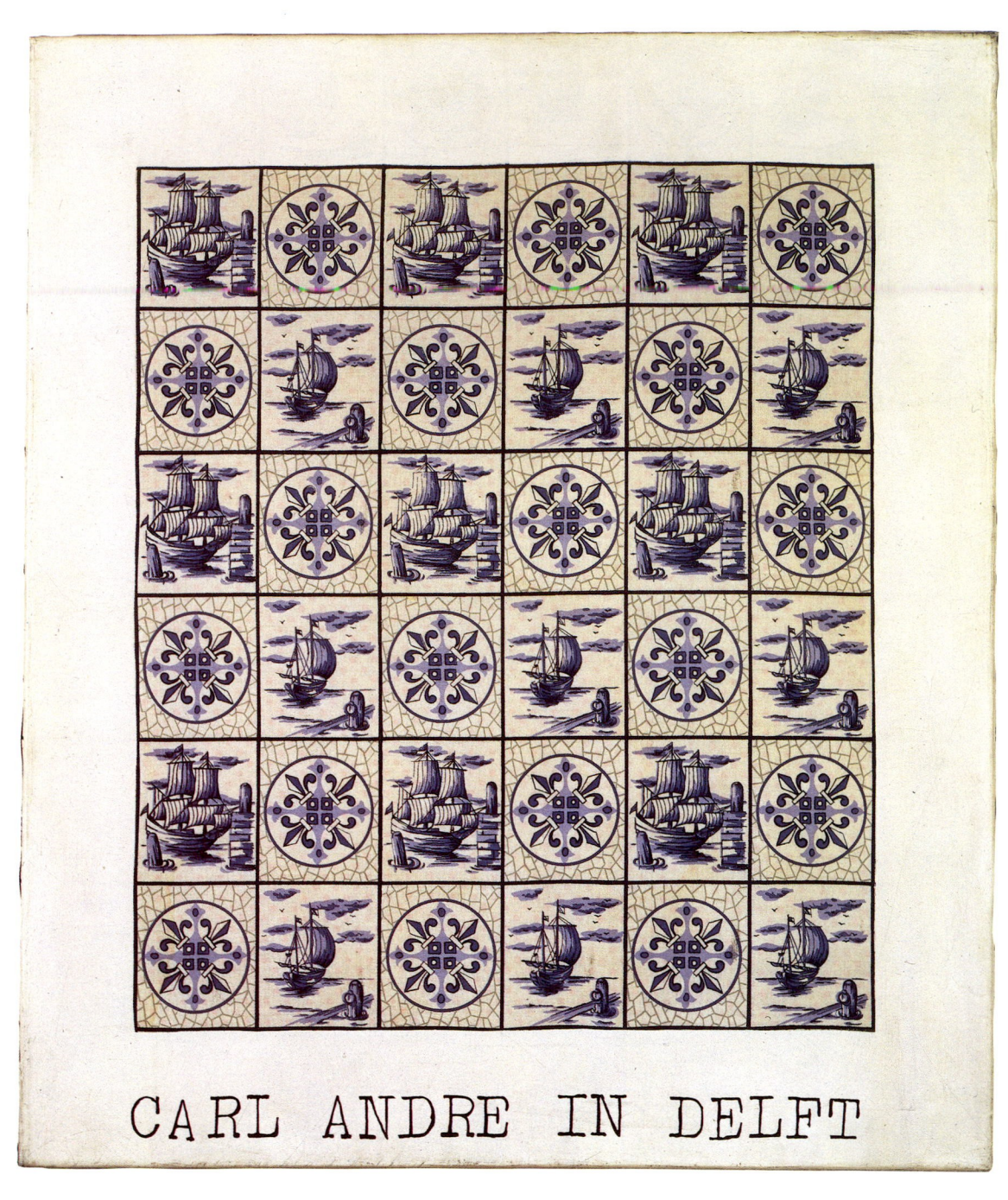

17. *Carl Andre in Delft* 1968

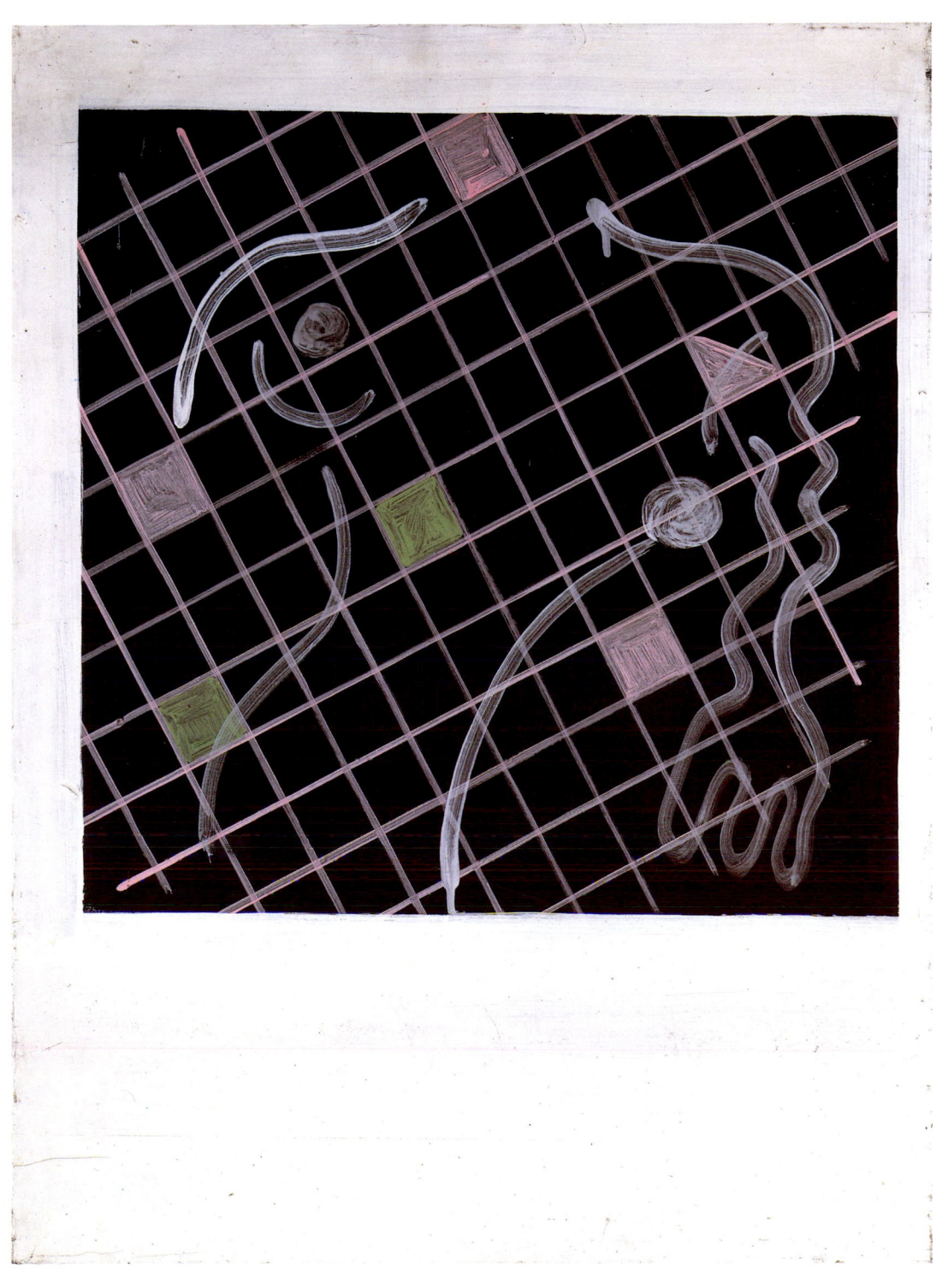

13. *Nude with Squares* 1966

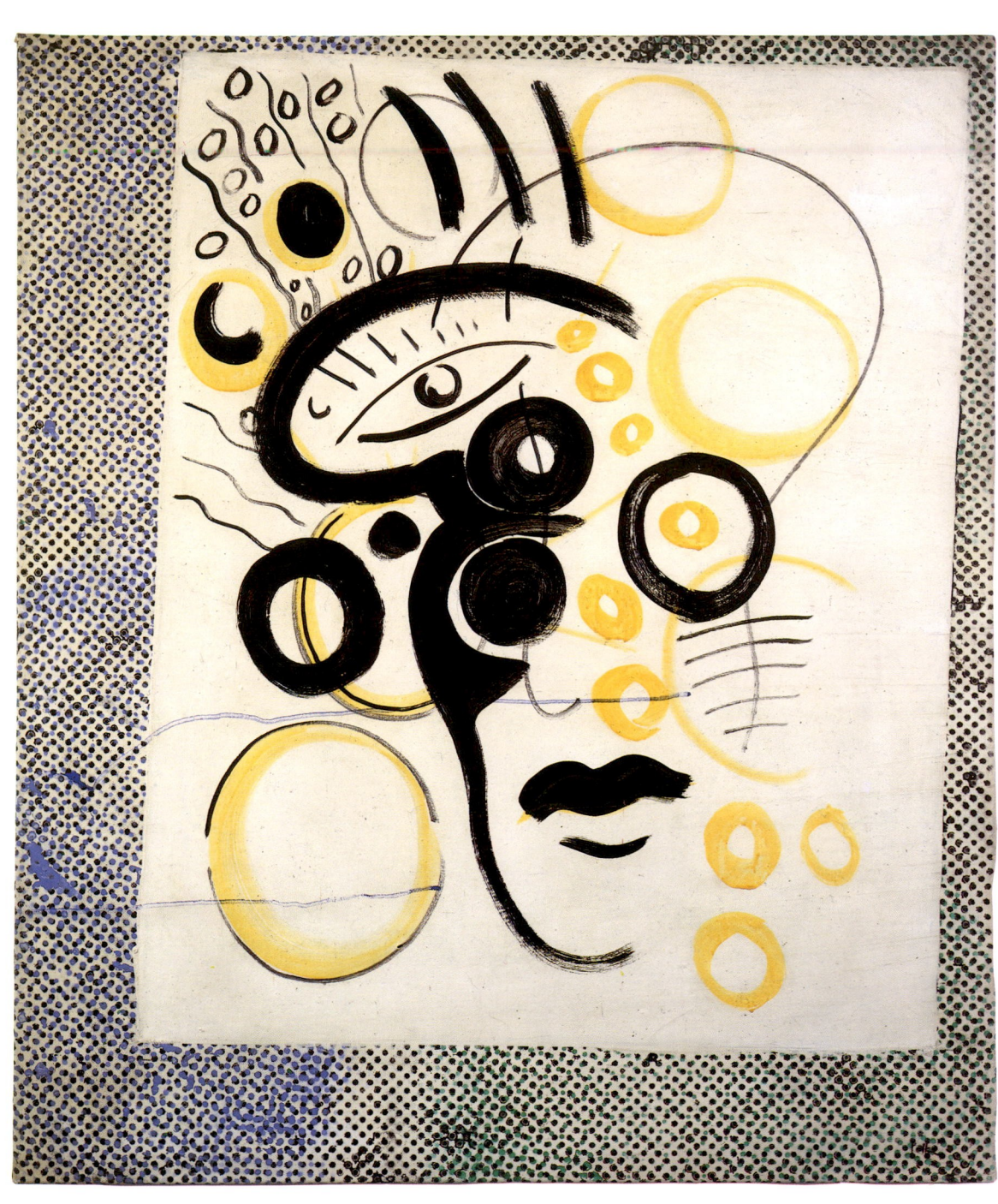

14. *Untitled (Head)* 1966–8

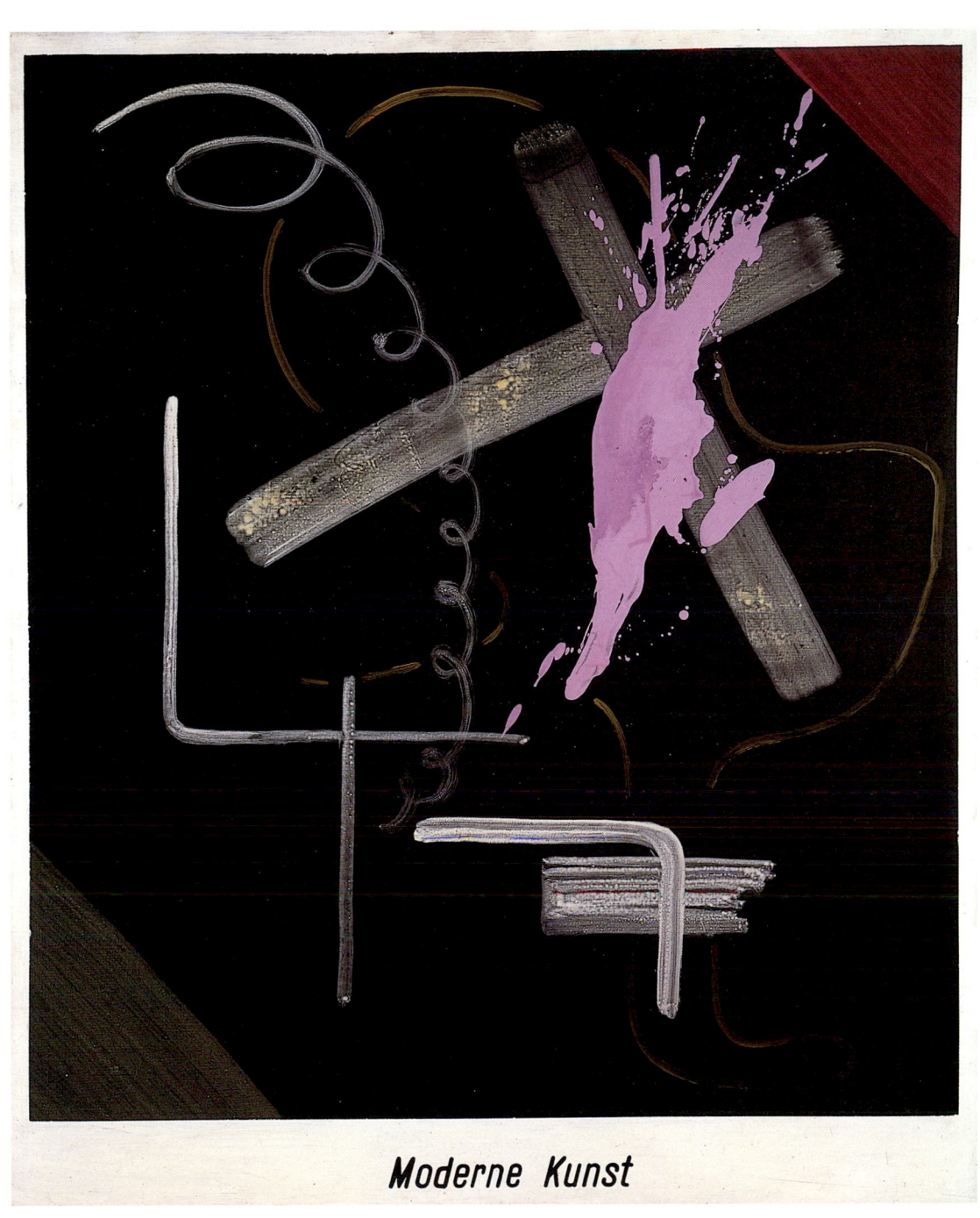

18. *Modern Art* 1968

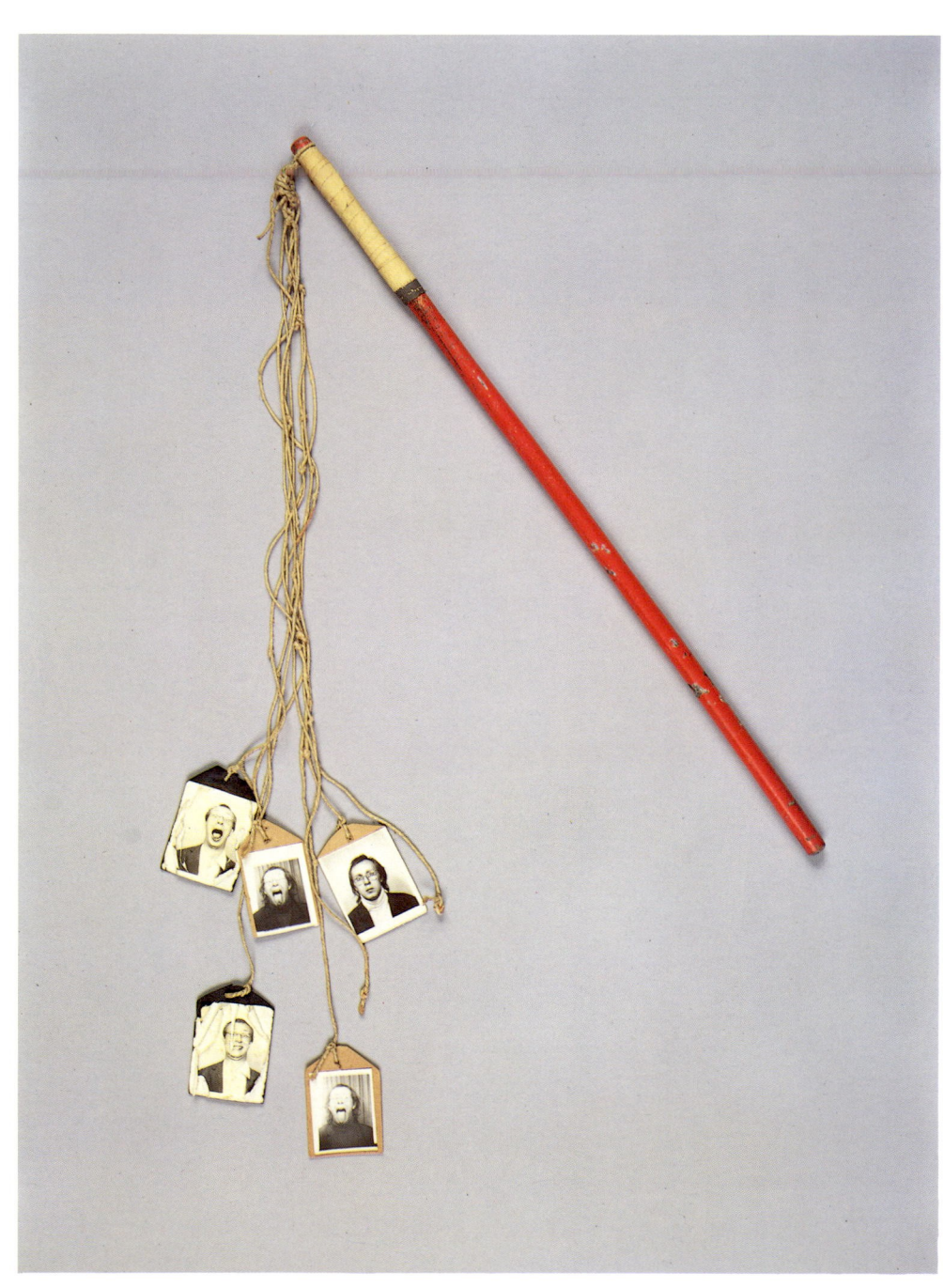

20. *Polke's Whip* 1968

1	+	1	=	3
2	+	3	=	6
4	+	4	=	5
7	+	3	=	8
5	+	1	=	2
3	+	4	=	9
6	+	2	=	7
8	+	7	=	4
1	+	5	=	2

16. *Solutions V* 1967

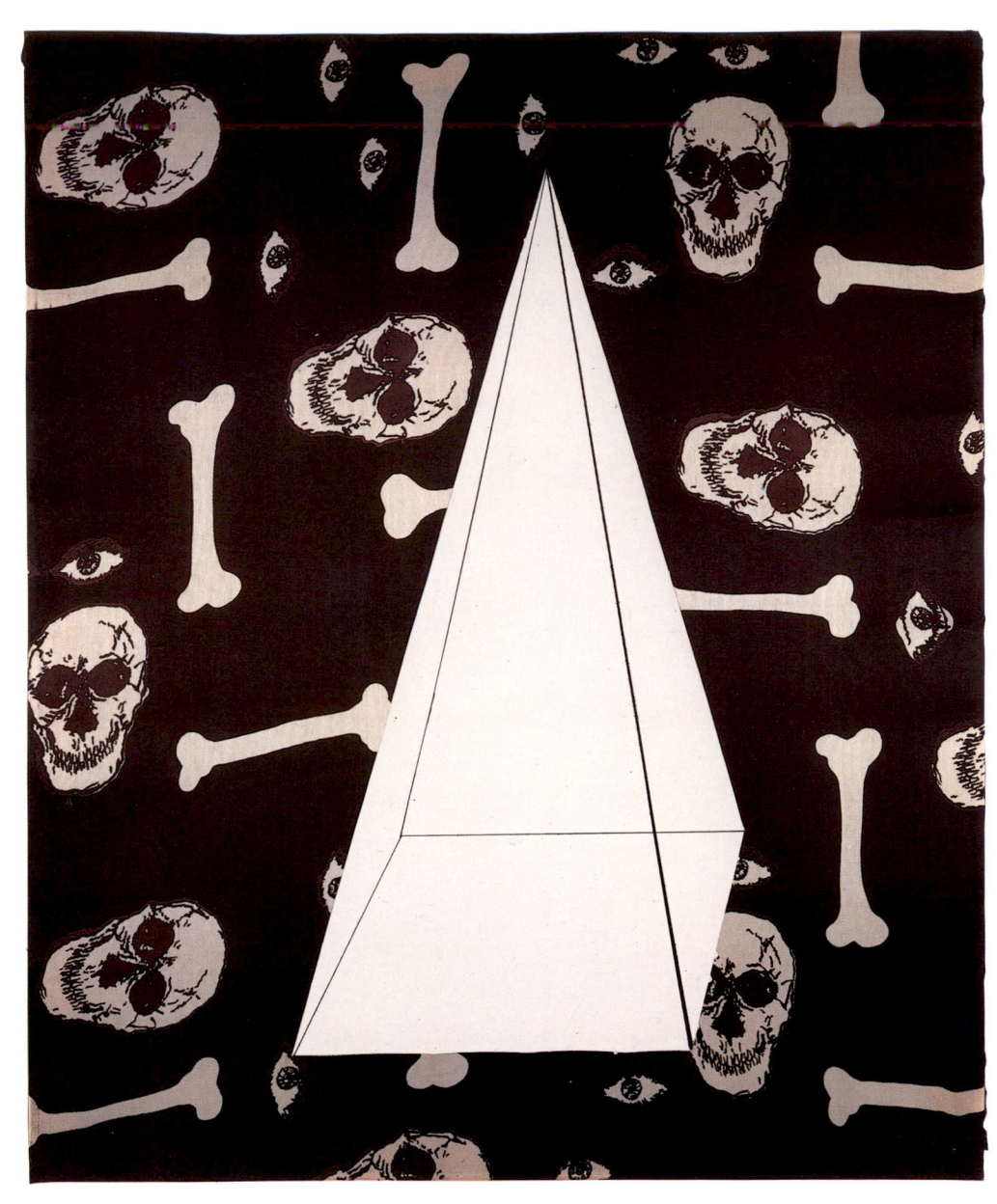

19. *White Obelisk* 1968

Höhere Wesen befahlen: rechte obere Ecke schwarz malen!

23. *The Higher Powers Command:*
    Paint the Right Hand Corner Black 1969

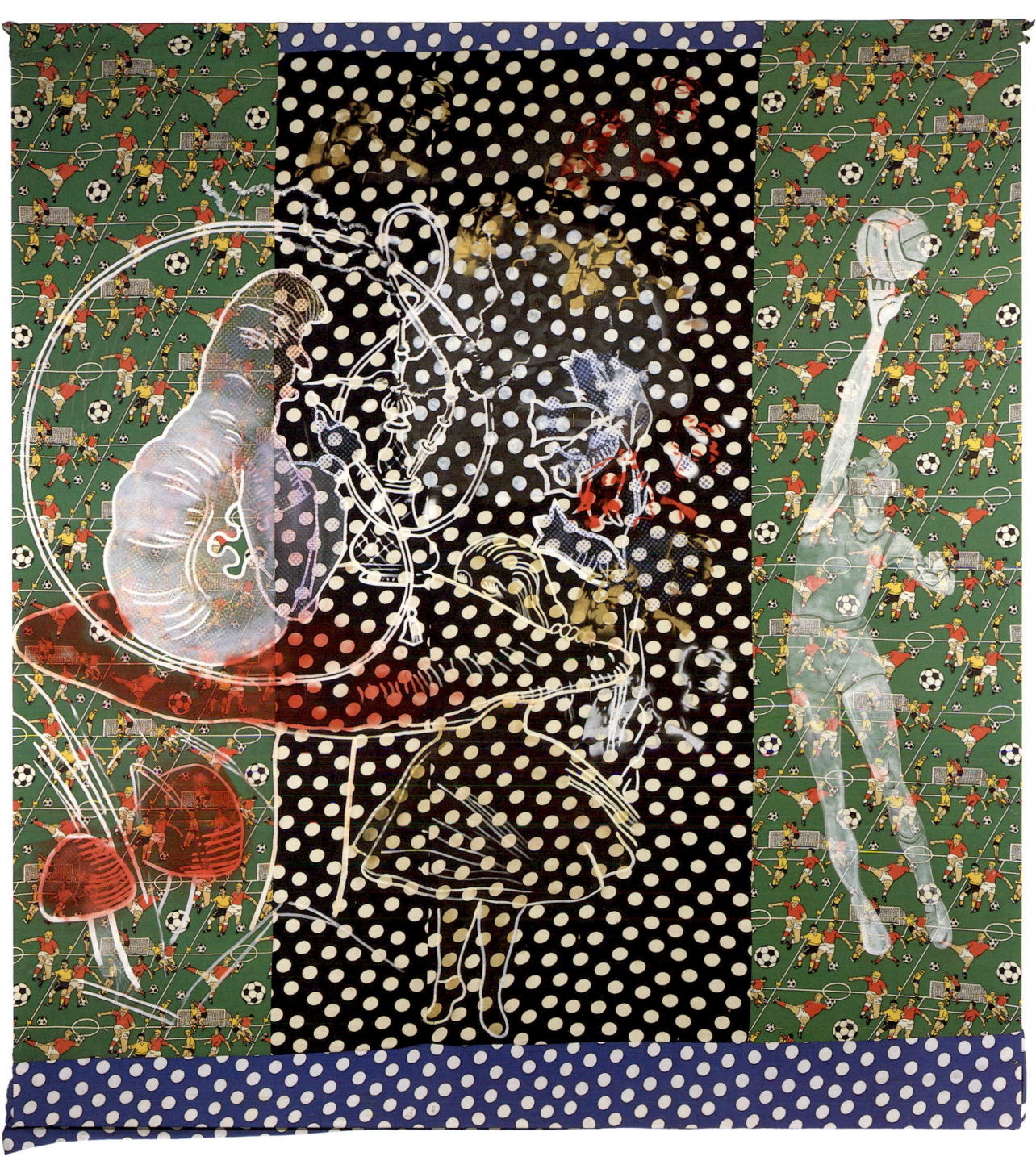

24. *Alice in Wonderland* 1971

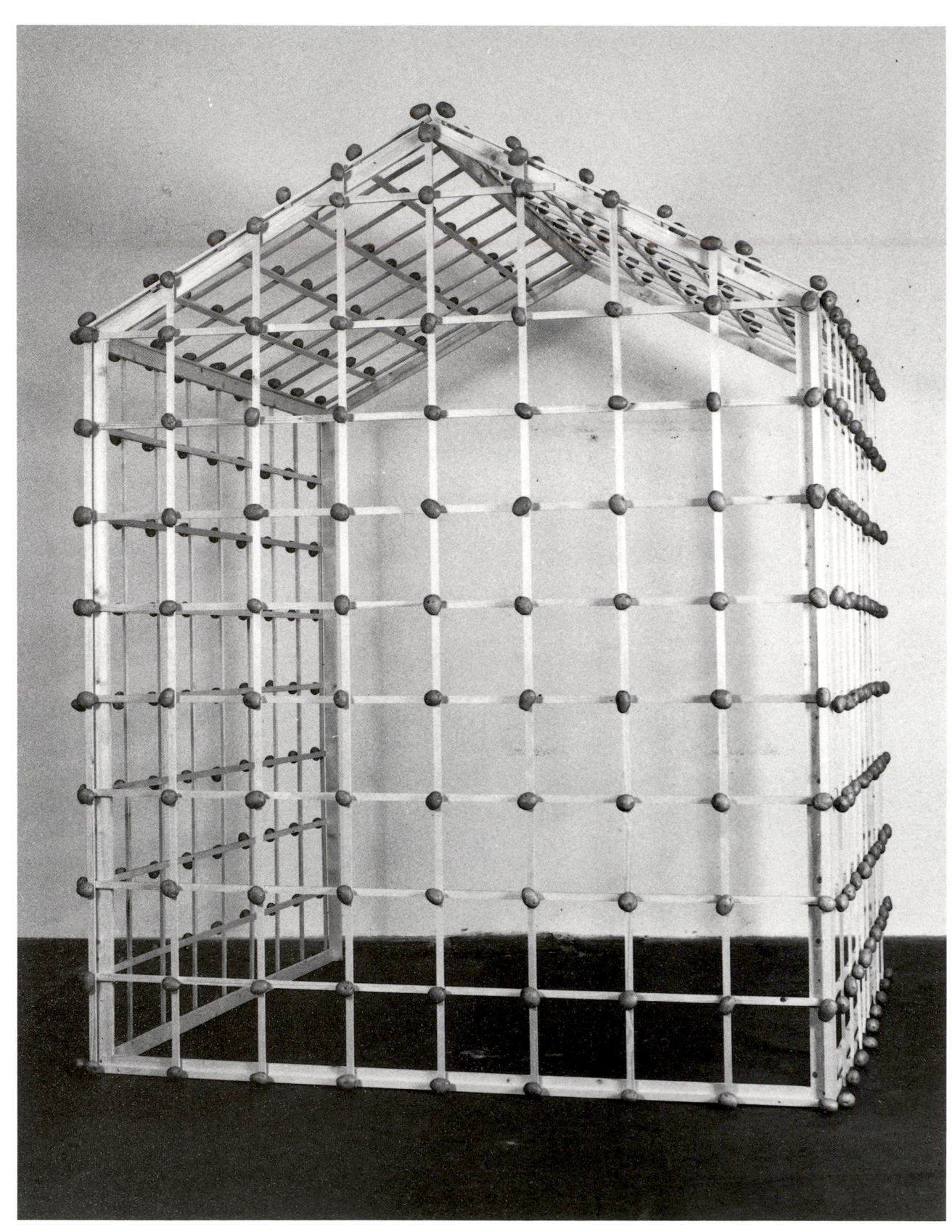

15. *Potato House* 1967 (second version 1990)

Potatology for Beginners

Judith Nesbitt

> Artists are the ecologists of homelessness, questioners of houses, dissident dwellers. Their residence among things means that they work with appearing forms – whether they stem from nature, culture or the cosmos of scientific signs and models. The house of the dissident dweller is filled with strange guests – it is a point in the lattice of the world, a magic number, a vantage point affording a view of garish colours.
>
> Peter Sloterdijk[1]

Imagine, if you will, a house with three walls and a pitched roof. It is made of wooden trellis and potatoes. This *Potato House* grew in Sigmar Polke's head; now it travels the world. It has been seen in Berlin, Zurich, New York and now in Liverpool. Designed to pack flat for easy transportation, the potatoes are provided at each port of call. The *Potato House* is a simple capsule, bare inside, its walls full of windows. It is not a cage, for no cage ever had one wall missing. This is the house of the 'dissident dweller'.

A thoughtful gesture on the part of the artist, the *Potato House* serves as a grounding device amid the fireworks and fabulous trails on which his work leads us. It is a temporary shelter from which to view the world, or the circling worlds of Polke's imagination. From inside this molecular structure, we can view the colliding elements in Polke's pictorial cosmos – whirling, hallucinogenic figments from the worlds of science, culture and nature. With a screen of potatoes as fixed coordinates, we can chart the movements of shooting stars and sausages, palm trees and reindeers, mapping our journey as we join the dots of the visible world. The potatoes themselves will join the dots, their eyes and tails sprouting with profligate energy around this anti-house of the artist.

Perhaps as a travel guide we should like to take with us, into our *Potato House*, the following account of smoking hashish in Marseilles, for it could as easily be the experience of a tripper through the universe of Polke's paintings:

'Space can expand, the ground tilt steeply, atmospheric sensations occur: vapour, an opaque heaviness in the air; colours grow brighter, more luminous; objects more beautiful, or else more lumpy and threatening...All this does not occur in a continuous development; rather, it is typified by a continual alteration of dreaming and waking states, a constant and finally exhausting oscillation between totally different worlds of consciousness'.[2]

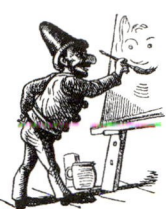

'Well if there is anything at all that manifests everything artists are supposed to be or have – the delight in innovation, creativity, spontaneity, productivity, creating entirely out of oneself and so on – then it is the potato'.

Sigmar Polke[3]

But you might ask: why a potato house and not a cauliflower house, for example? While other artists looked to Mount Parnassus for inspiration, Sigmar Polke looked to the potato field, and found there an unlikely emblem of the artist's creativity. Is it possible that like the hero in Gunter Grass' novel, *The Tin Drum*, Polke was born in a potato field? With inimitable wit, he has identified himself with the most common vegetable. Yet, as Katharina Schmidt has observed, in his work 'the potato, that universal food, amorphous in form, plain in appearance, humble in proportion to its powers, appears as the quintessential symbol of creative energy'.[4]

Polke chooses his emblems wisely. Just as Beuys used fat as a token of transformative energies, so Polke has used the potato. A joke at Beuys' expense or ours? The joke is not lost on the artist himself. Although the plainest and least shapely of vegetables, the potato has an irrepressible regenerative capacity. As Polke sees it, the potato creates entirely out of itself. It can be sexually propagated from seed, or non-sexually from the tuber. The 'eyes' themselves are the source of reproductive activity – a compelling metaphor for any artist, and especially one for whom the self-generated image is a recurring aspect of his practice. Polke's eyes would indeed seem to grow on stalks.

Polke has also played teasingly on the stupidity ascribed to potatoes in the German word 'Kartoffelkopf', in a series of 'Potato-Head' drawings of the mid-1960s. The vegetable's amorphous shape is a gift to the artist who can readily transform it – a potato becomes a potato-head in one swerve of Polke's hand. In one drawing (p50), a male and female potato-head engage in a little night-time flirtation, the delicacy of the colours sympathetically drawn from the palette of the

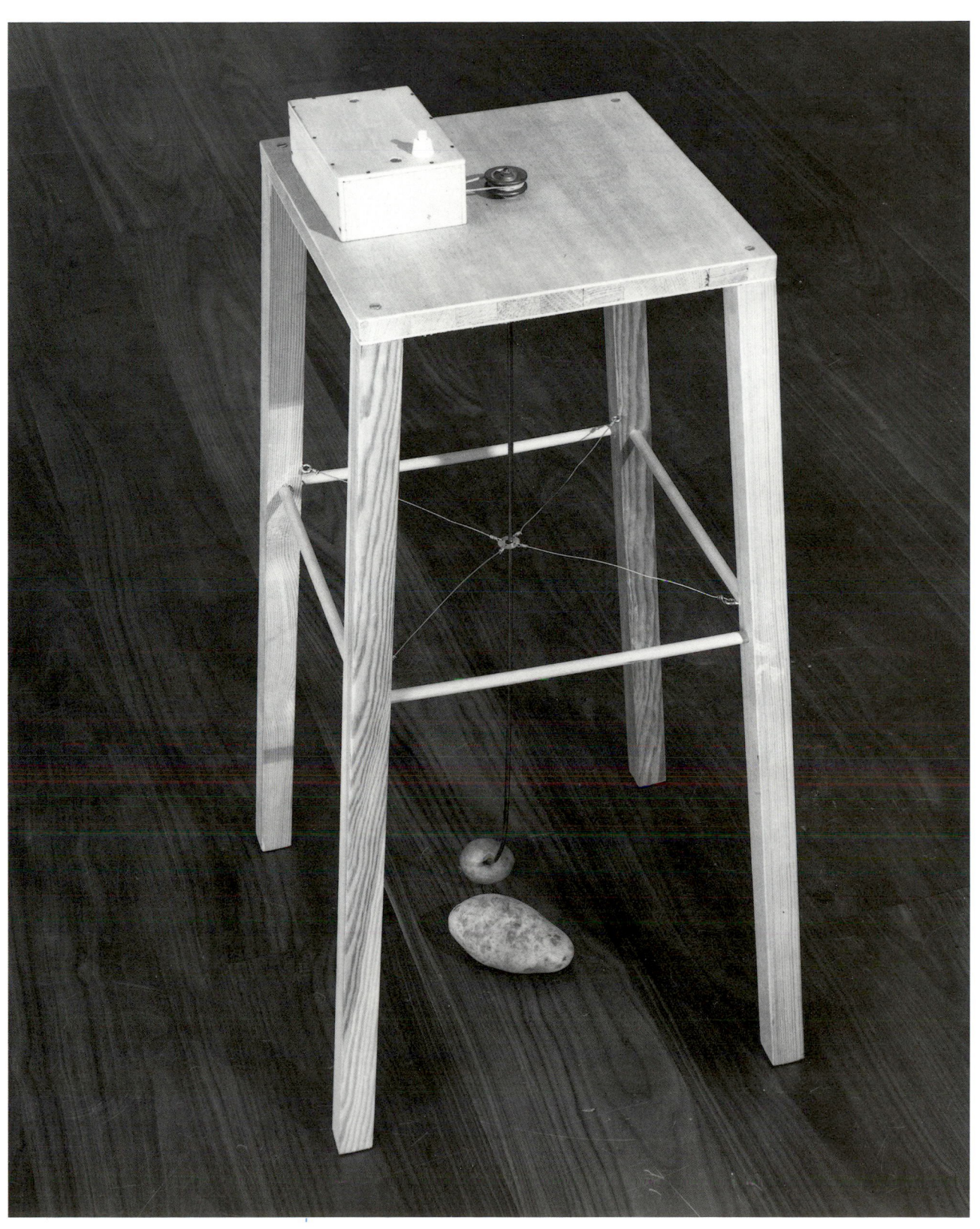

Potato Machine 1969, edition 22/30, wood, metal, motor, potatoes, Michael Werner Gallery, New York

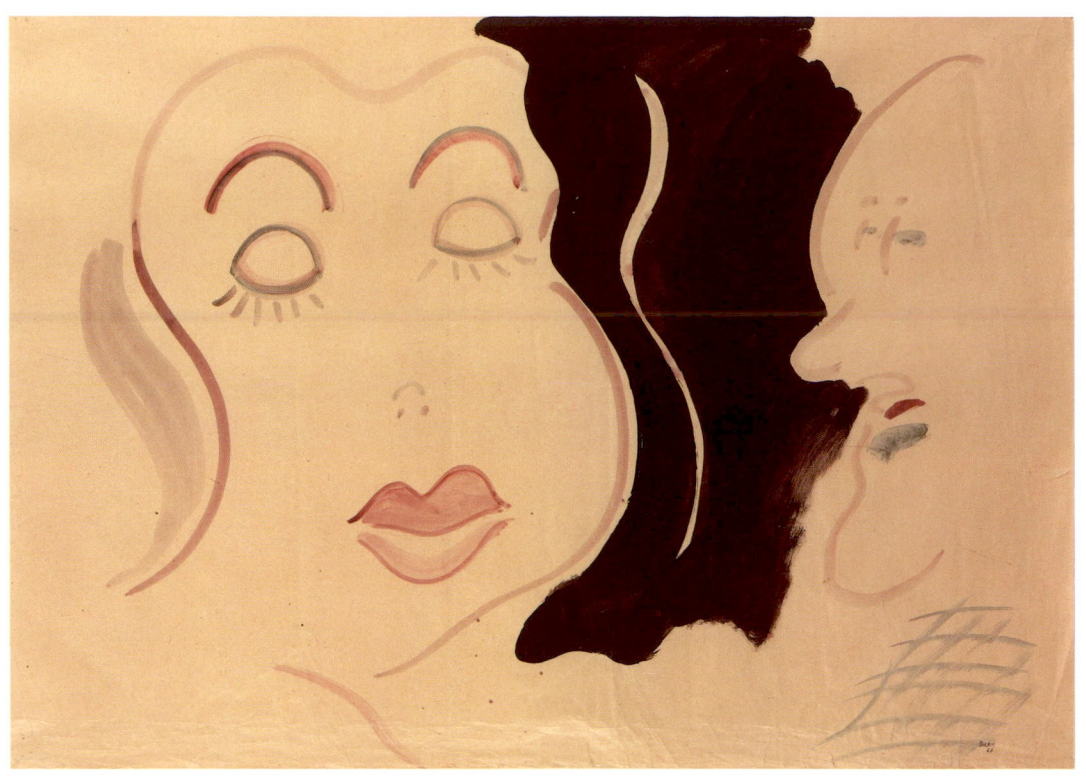

Untitled 1966, gouache and watercolour, Private Collection, London

vegetable itself. In another, *Untitled (Kiss, Kiss)* 1965 (p51), a male potato-head, featureless other than for his eyes which bulge with shock, is patterned with the lipstick of a predatory female.

And who else but Polke would invent a *Potato Machine* 1969 (p49), an ingenious adaptation of a domestic stool? On pressing the button, one potato orbits round another, which is set, like the sun, at the centre of the cosmos under the stool.

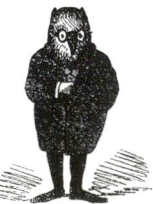

What, meanwhile, of the Potato House dweller, following Polke's maverick journey in real time, to land in Liverpool, city of the Beatles, football and maritime history?

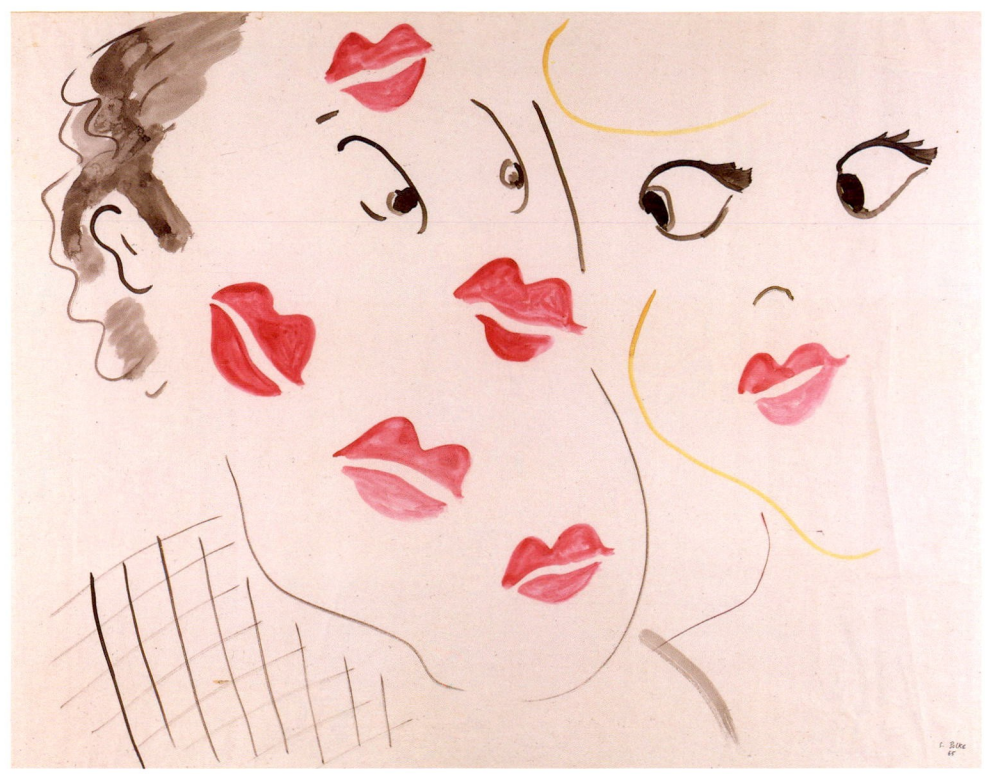

Untitled (Kiss, Kiss) 1965, gouache and watercolour on paper, Collection Speck, Cologne

Perhaps the Higher Powers have directed the journey, with the same perverse logic with which they have governed the artist's subjects. Some hand has joined the dots between Liverpool and Cologne (Polke's adopted city), pairing them like sauerkraut and chips. For, in a move that the Higher Powers themselves must have commanded, the city of Liverpool was formally twinned with Cologne in 1952. For all the pairing of two European ports, few would see in Liverpool the 'double' of Cologne; it is more obviously its poor relation. But there was inspiration in the link-up, for Liverpool offers much to an artist such as Polke, and to viewers, a fitting temporary site for the *Potato House*.

Visiting Polke in Cologne, I took with me, as gifts, two little pocketbooks: *Lern yerself Scouse: How to talk proper in Liverpool*, Volumes 1 and 3. The intermediate Volume 2 was either sold out or never printed, but with a willing pupil like Polke, this proved no obstacle. We spent the rest of the evening rehearsing such essential phrases for the visitor to Liverpool as…'Wersia sensa yuma?' – much to the consternation of the other diners in the restaurant. Besides a 'sensa yuma', Polke shares with Liverpool his interest in the potato; for 'scouse' – the generic name for all things Liverpudlian, the humour, dialect, and character – derives, in fact, from the potato. Historians record that:

> The infiltration of the potato into Lancashire was rapid and widespread, as early as 1700. At the same time, one hears of 'lobscouse', a highly flavoured dish of potato, meat and onions, associated particularly with the seamen of the Lancashire ports. So popular was lobscouse that Ned Ward declares that 'the ship's cook has sent the fellow a thousand times to the Devil that ever invented Lobscouse.
>
> Redcliffe Salaman[5]

'Lobscouser' came to be a nickname for sailors, just as 'scouser' became a nickname for the people of Liverpool.

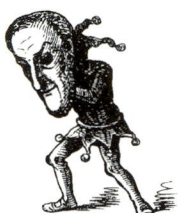

The potato can justly claim to be a universal food. It is still grown where it originated on some of the highest inhabited plains in the world, in the mountain villages of Bolivia and Peru. There it is the core of existence and ritual life. As traditionally in Ireland, so also in Peru, a meal without a potato is not a meal. The centrality of the potato to the Amarayan people of Bolivia has given rise to a proverb:

> 'Without potatoes [we] would be like loose threads on a loom, for potatoes are what bind life together'.[6]

The potato has been the subject of a monumental work of scholarship, published in 1949 and now a classic (proof, if it were needed, that Polke and the present writer are not the only potato-heads). The author of *The History and Social Influence of the Potato*, R N Salaman, ranges boldly across many disciplines, to show how the potato is inextricably bound with centuries of human histories. Ireland occupies almost a third of the acreage in this 700-page history, but 'The Potato in Tristan da Cunha' has a chapter to itself (XXVIII). Alas, Salaman wrote his epic history just too soon to take account in his chapter 'The Potato in the Realm of Art' of the work of Sigmar Polke (but could not fail to make mention of Van Gogh's seminal *Potato Eaters*). Therefore, for budding potatologists, I offer here some facts from the life of the potato, nuggets of history, like the potato itself. They are dug, for the most part, from Salaman's epic study:

- First cultivated 2000 years ago, the potato came to Europe from South America (if not in Walter Raleigh's bags then in someone else's – most probably a Spaniard). Peru was its main source, where the potato grew wild. (Lima, Peru is today the home of the International Potato Centre).

- In seventeenth century Europe, the potato was a luxury food for aristocrats, for it had not yet proved its worth as a high yielding plant and, troubled with disease, remained a marginal and expensive vegetable. As late as 1716 the potato was considered less important than the radish!

- Marie Antoinette wore potato flowers in her hair to celebrate the arrival of the potato in France.

- By the end of the eighteenth century, Liverpool's potato trade was flourishing to the extent that it exported its surplus to Dublin.

- Some saw in the potato 'the most fruitful root we have; its fructifying quality is visible in every cabbin you pass by. They produce good soldiers, good seamen, good citizens and good husbandmen'.

- Doctors recommended the potato as an aid to fecundity: 'Doctor Lloyd whose eminence as a physician was very great, frequently recommended potatoes as a supper to those ladies whom providence had not blessed with children, and an heir has often been the consequence'.

- Salaman writes that 'a series of bad wheat and rye harvests on the Continent had been followed by famine conditions in 1770. This was countered by so great an increase in the production of potatoes that...it looked as if it might assume a similar role in Europe, as rice had for centuries done in China'.

- The War of the Bavarian Succession, 1778-9, known in German history as the 'Kartoffelkreig', ended only when the opposing armies had eaten all the available potatoes in Bavaria.

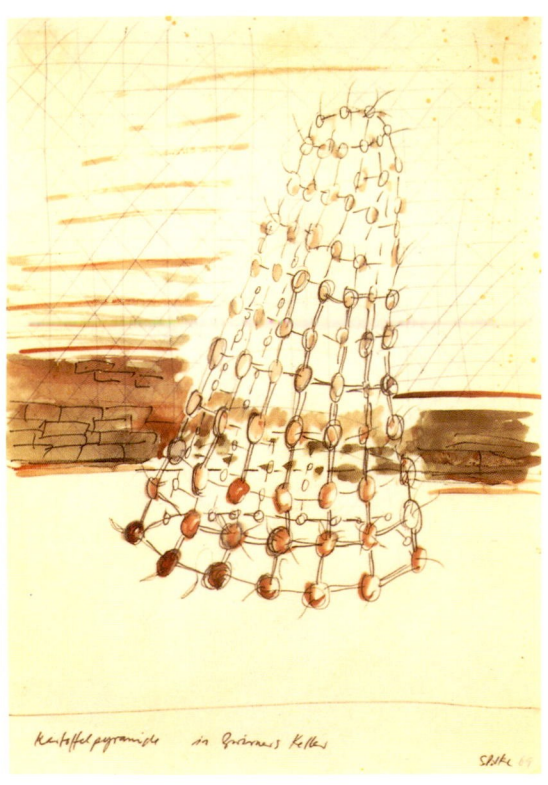

Potato Pyramid in Zwirner's Cellar 1969, ballpoint pen, watercolour and Rapidograph on paper, Private Collection

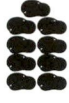 'As soon as the potato was established [in Ireland], the standard of living automatically became fixed at a level commensurate with the energy its production demanded... As time went on, the sequence – poverty, potatoes, larger families, more potatoes, and greater poverty, became ever more firmly established, till nothing but revolution or catastrophe could break it'.

 In the Irish potato famine of 1845-9, one million people died, and another million emigrated, many of them coming to Liverpool in search of food, and, if they could afford it, a passage to America. In 1847, as the famine reached its worst stage, Liverpool was flooded with Irish emigrants, who broke into cellars to find shelter – 40 people were found occupying one cellar. Legislation ensued, but the Irish protested that they would rather die in Liverpool than be deported to die in Ireland. Cellar dwellers were removed eighty at a time, and the cellars were filled up with sand.

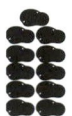 For the entire year of 1910, a Danish researcher lived on a diet of only potatoes, and was fit and well at the end of the year.

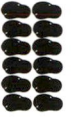 In the media coverage of the 1992 US presidential election campaign, Dan Quayle, Vice-President elect, revealed to the assembled world's press and a class of primary schoolchildren that he couldn't spell potato, insisting, to a bemused boy who had written the word correctly on the blackboard, that his 'potato' was missing an 'e'.

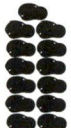 The humble potato has chosen an illustrious line of artists through whom to make its contribution to the history of art, among them Van Gogh, Joan Miró and Paul Klee. Not least among these is Sigmar Polke who, at an impressionable age, picked up the potato and saw in it an emblem of the irrepressible energies of art, and life itself.

1. Peter Sloterdijk, *Sigmar Polke*, Amsterdam, 1992, p55.

2. Joël and Fränkel, 'Der Haschisch-Rausch', Klinische Wochenschrift, 1926, vol 5, p37. Quoted by Walter Benjamin as a 'preliminary remark' to 'Hashish in Marseilles' in *One Way Street and Other Writings*, London and New York, 1979, p215.

3. Quoted in Walter Grasskamp, 'Illuminations in the Darkroom', *Art and Design*, 1989, nos 9-10, pp51-3.

4. Katharina Schmidt, *Sigmar Polke*, San Francisco, 1991, p37.

5. Redcliffe Salaman, *The History and Social Influence of the Potato*, Cambridge, 1949, reprinted 1986, p17.

6. Mick Johnsson, *Food and Culture among the Bolivian Aymara: symbolic expressions of social relations*, Uppsala, 1966, p79.

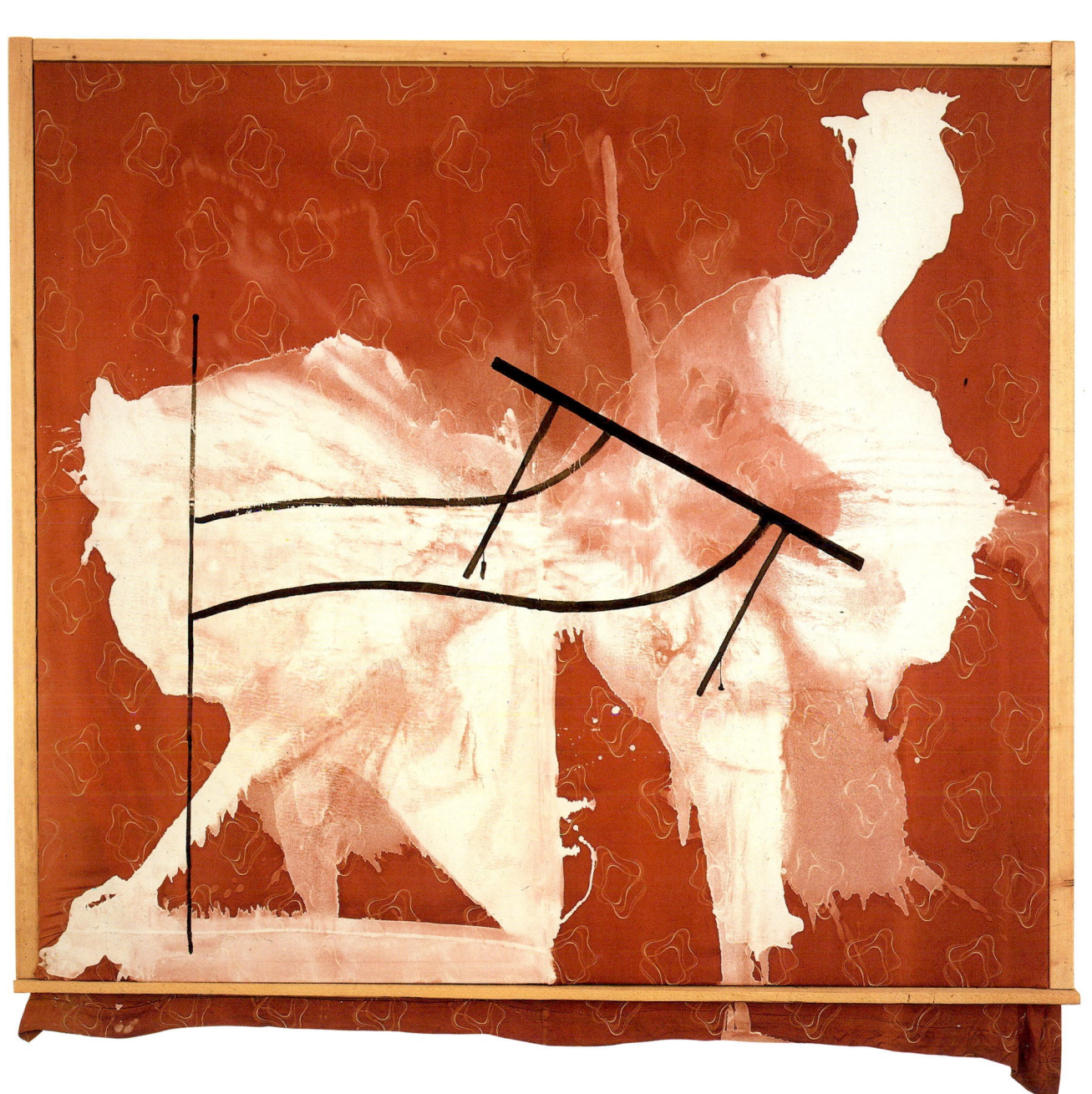

25. *Table Turning* 1981

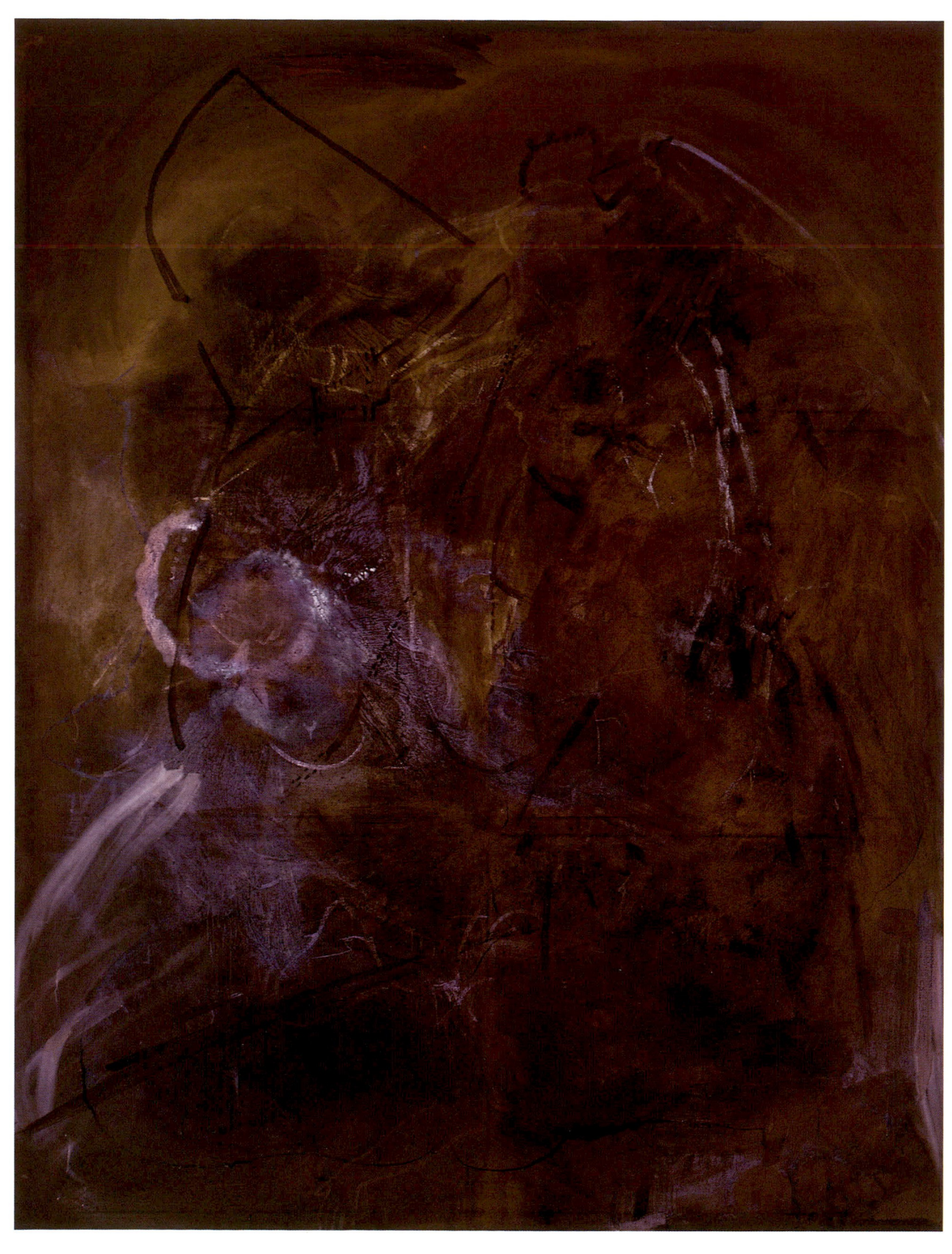

31. *Negative Value I: Alkor* 1982

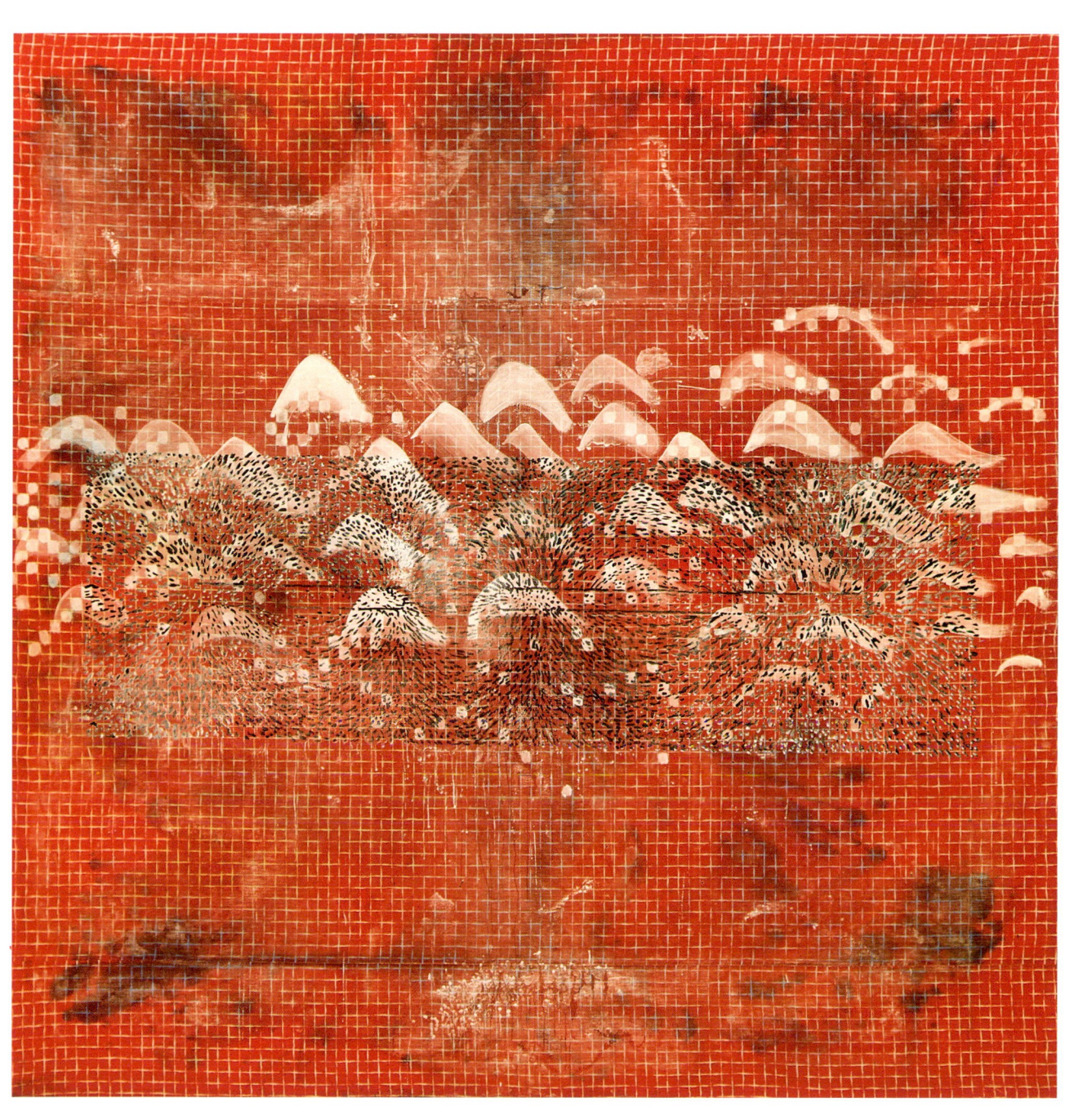

28. *Magnetic Landscape* 1982

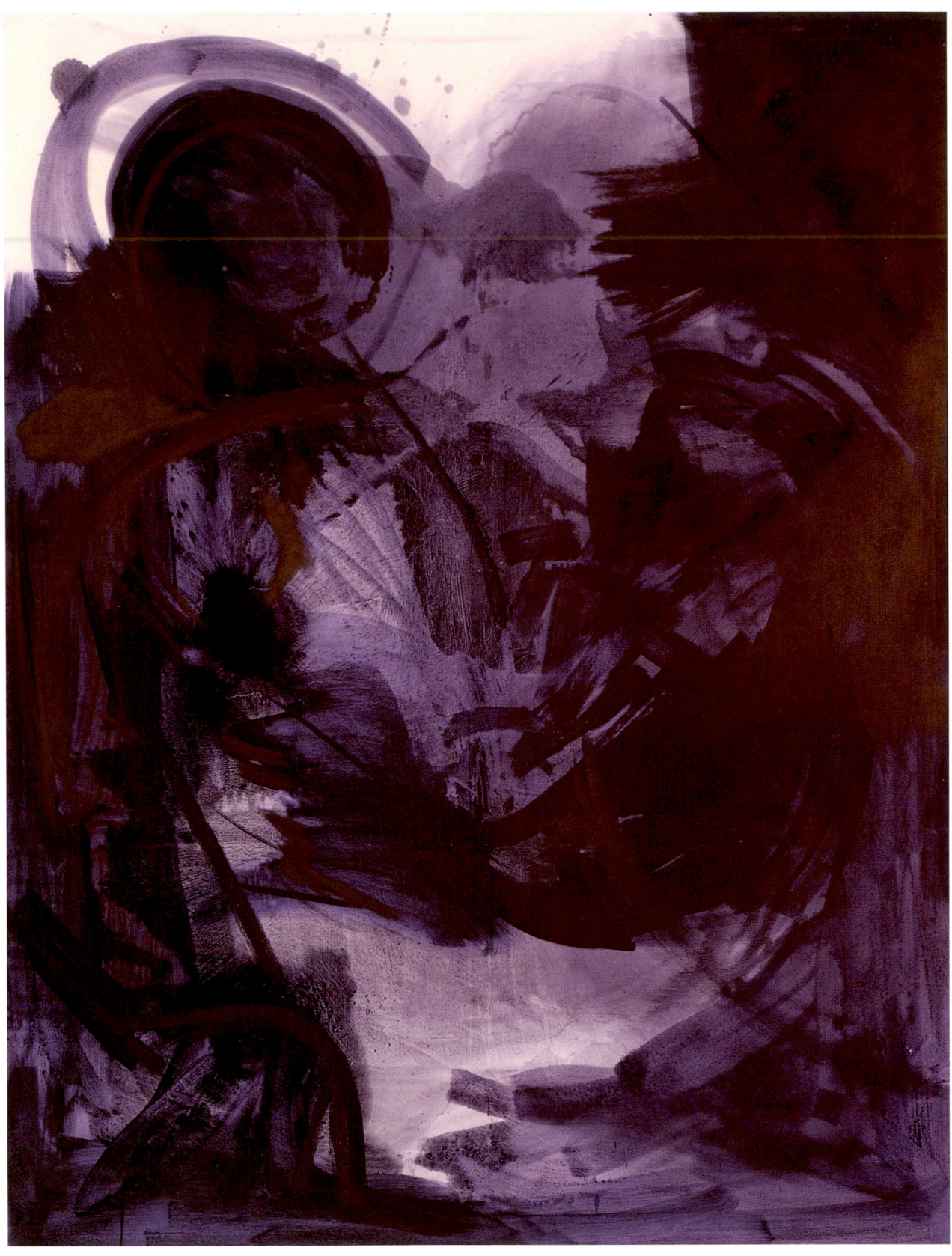

32. *Negative Value II: Mizar* 1982

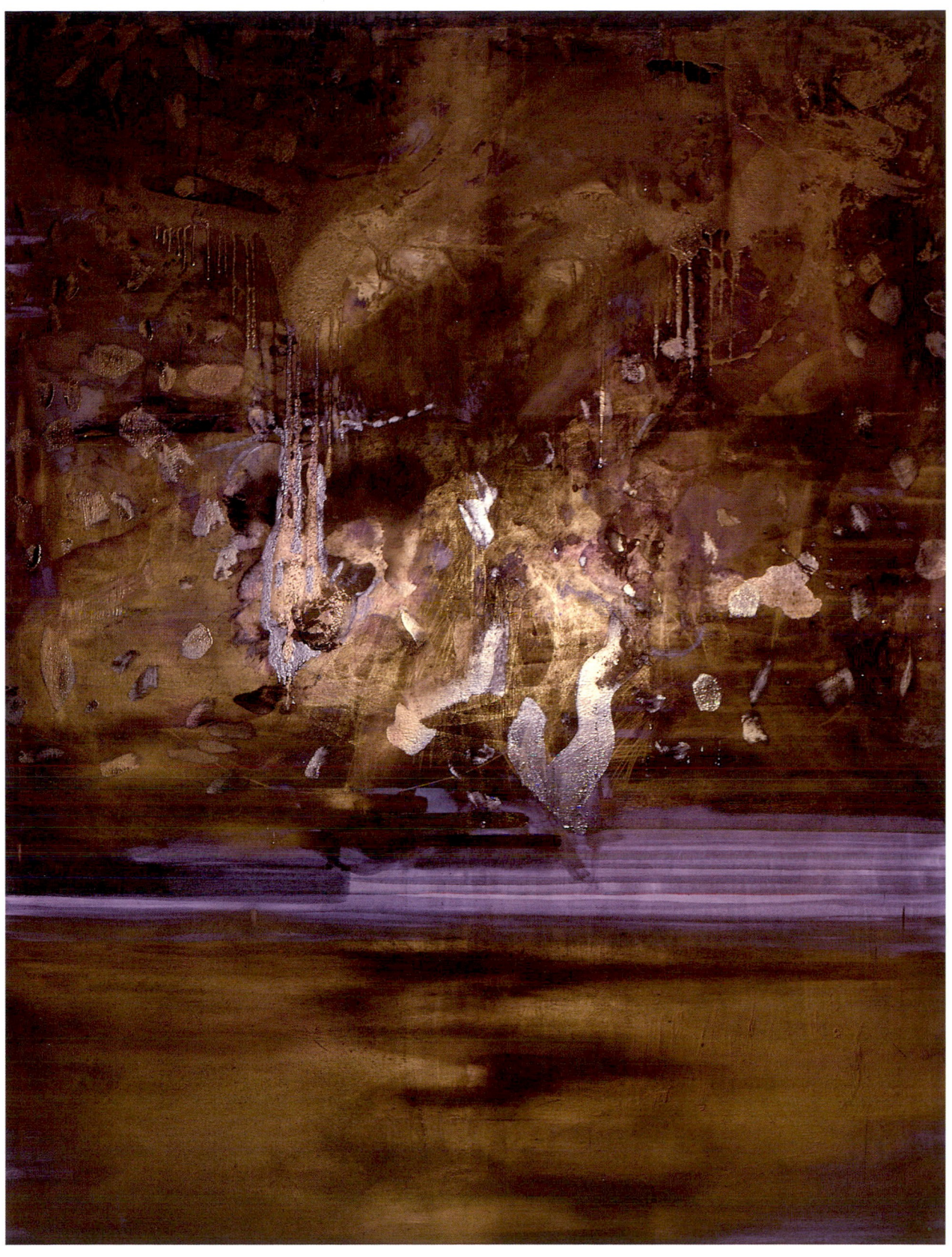

33. *Negative Value III: Aldebaran* 1982

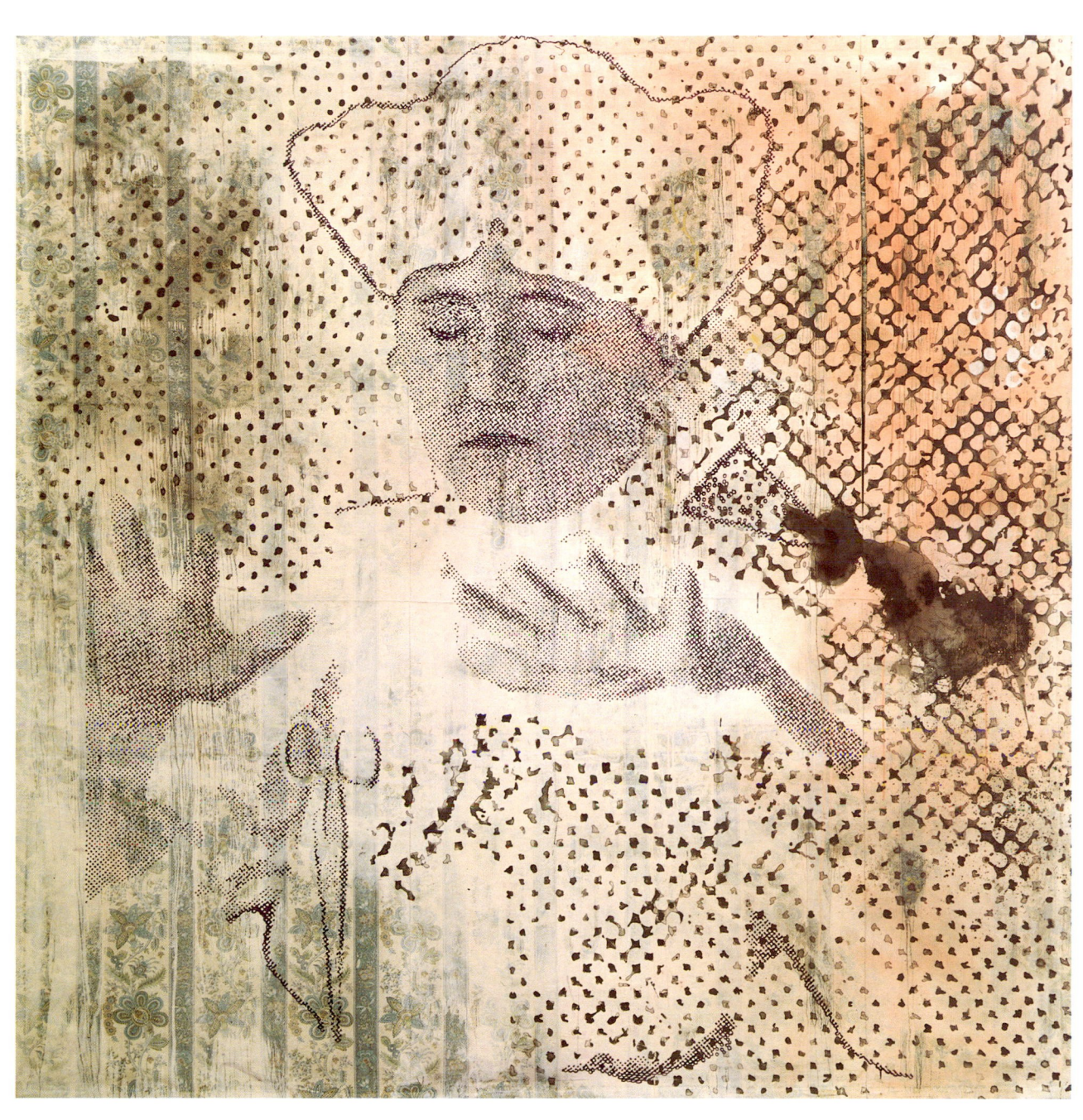

27. *Scissors* 1982

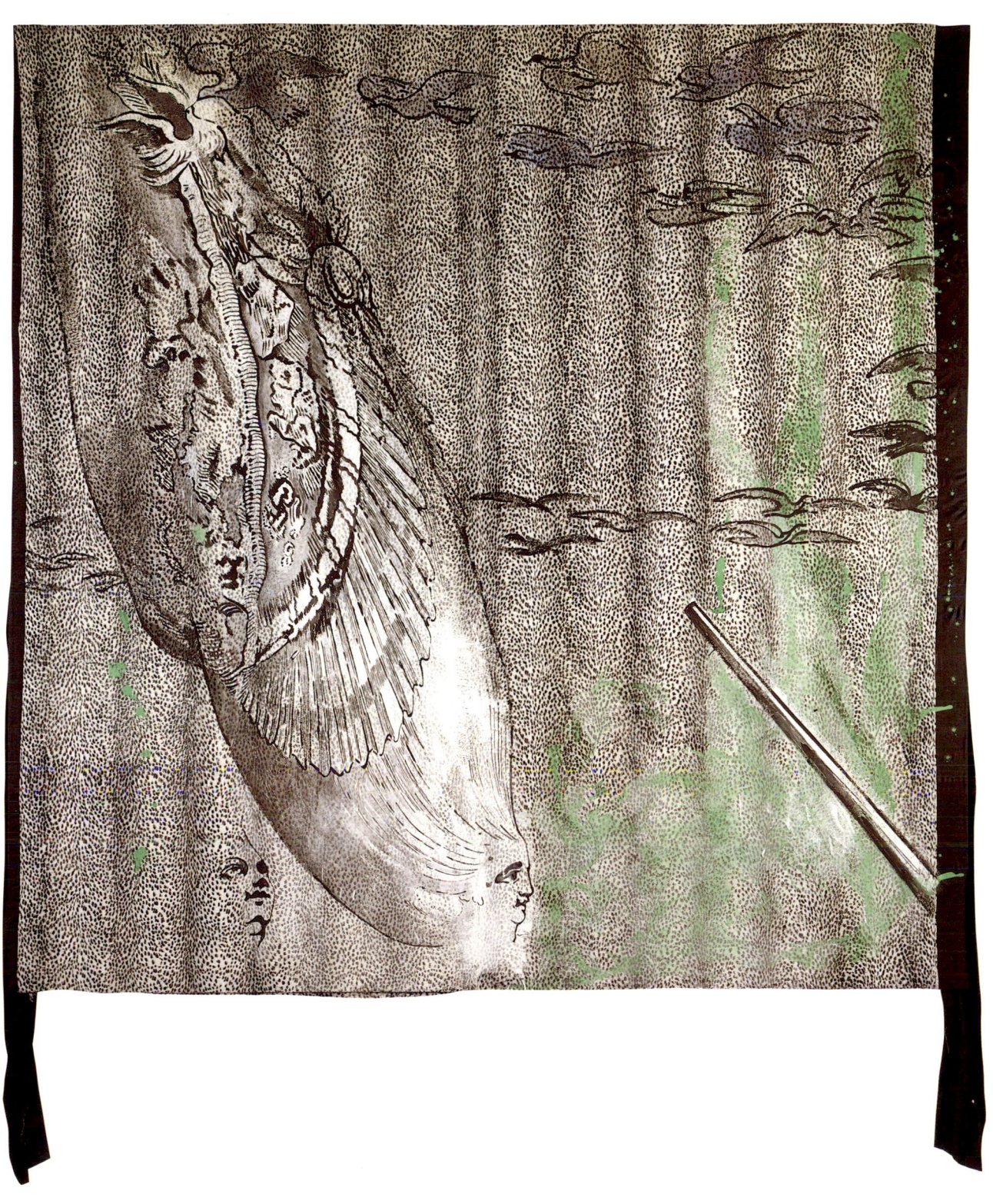

41. *Wig* 1983

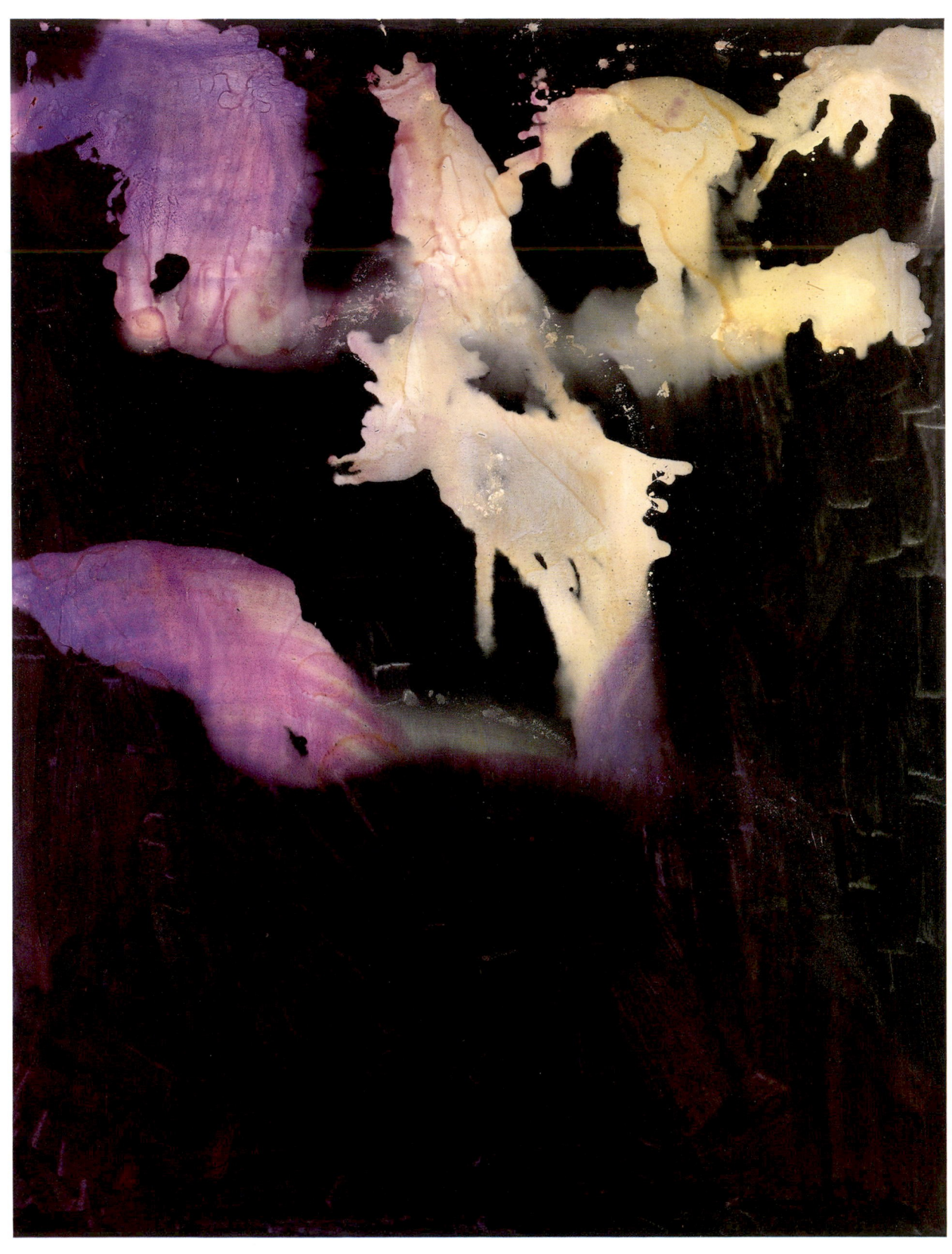

49. *Untitled (Spots)* 1986

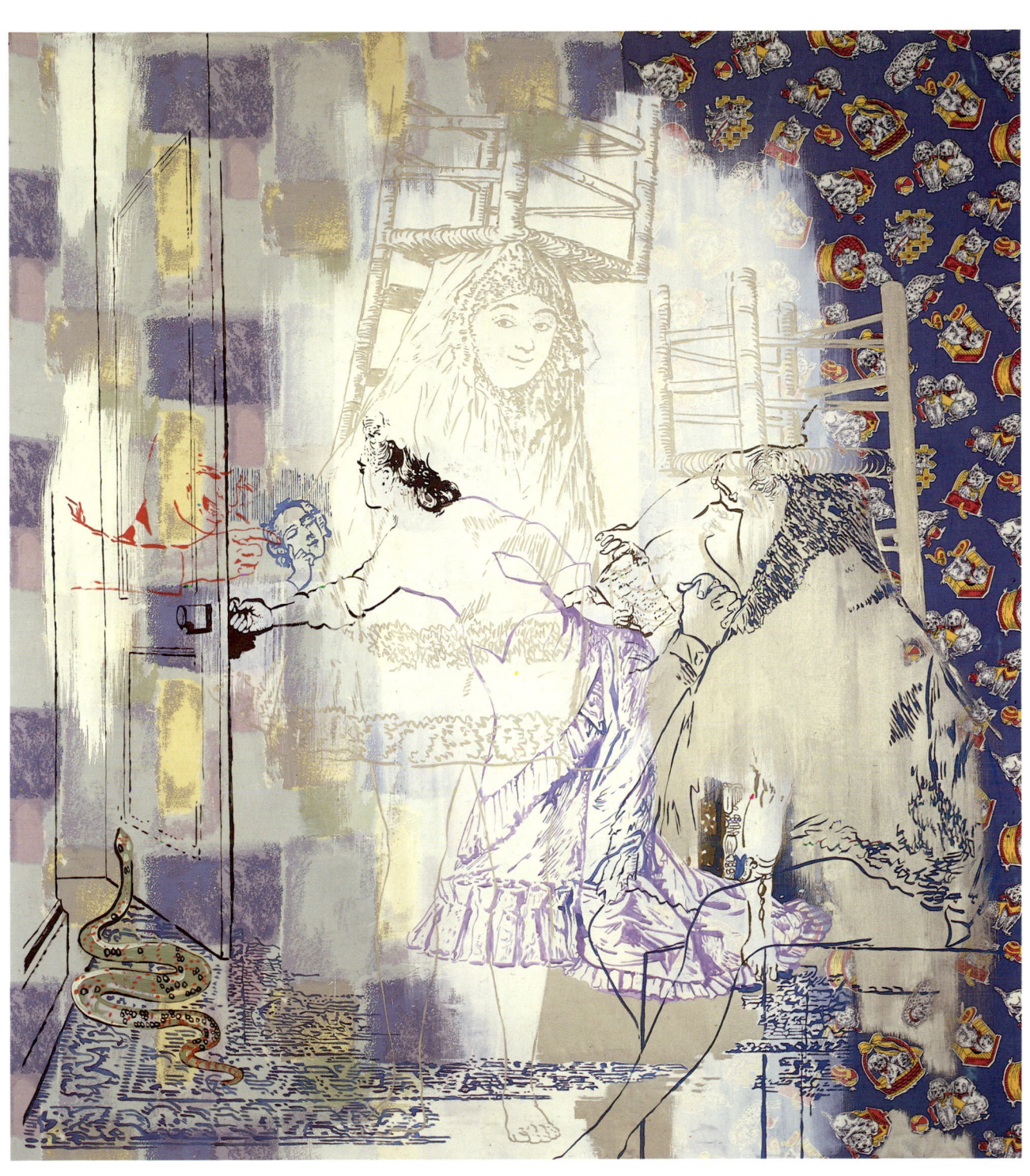

39. *This is how you sit correctly (after Goya)* 1982

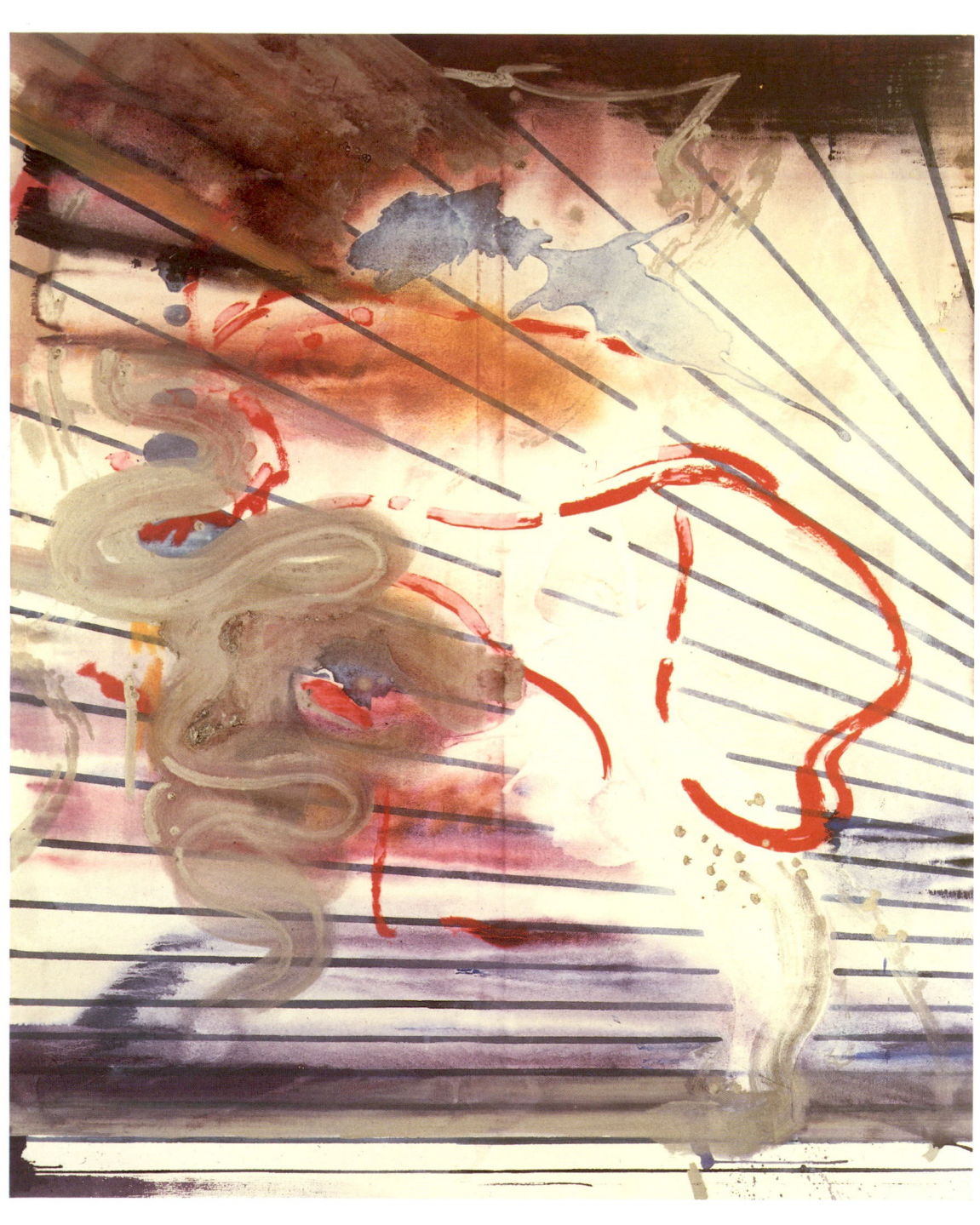

29. *Landscape* 1982

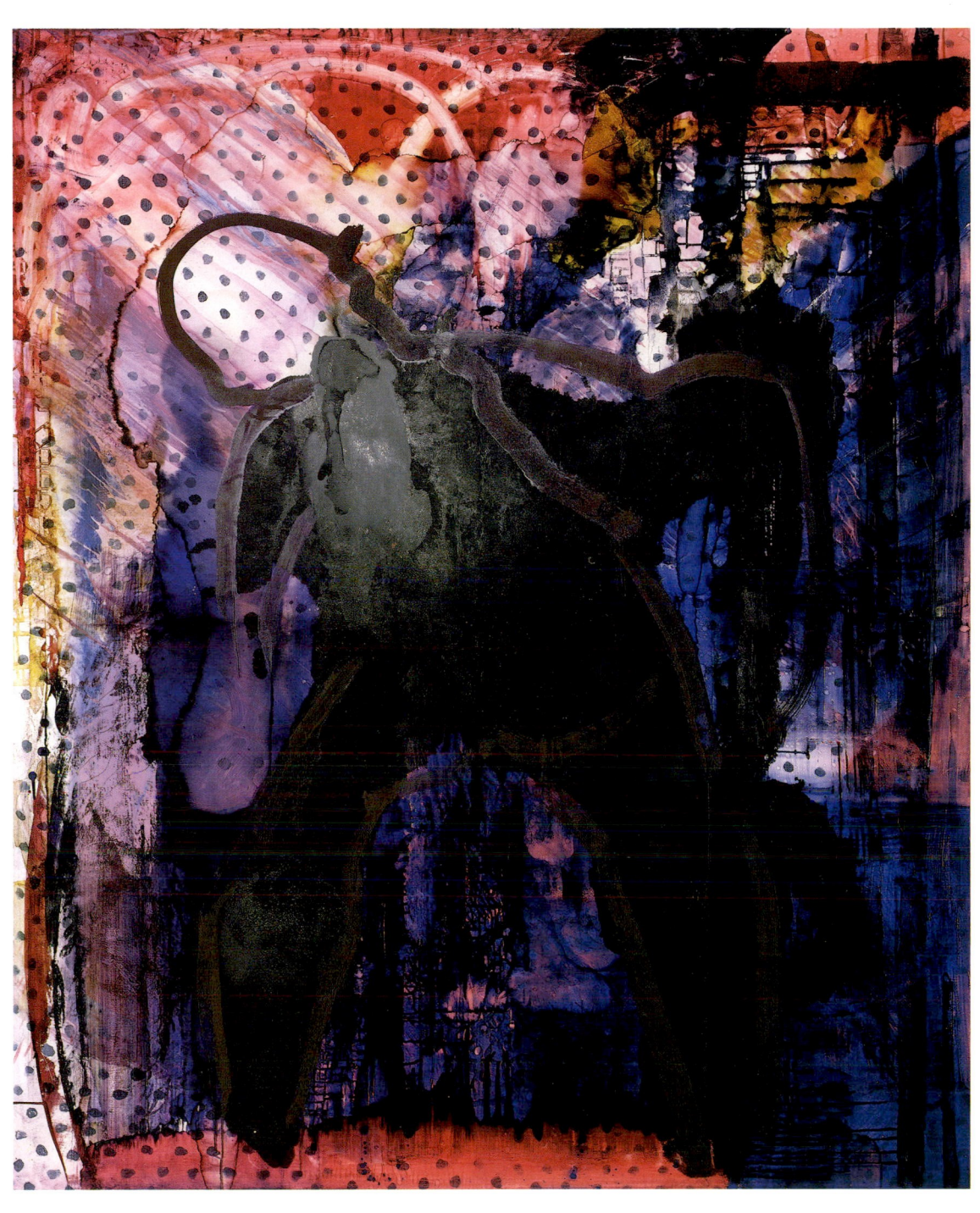

30. *Black Man* 1982

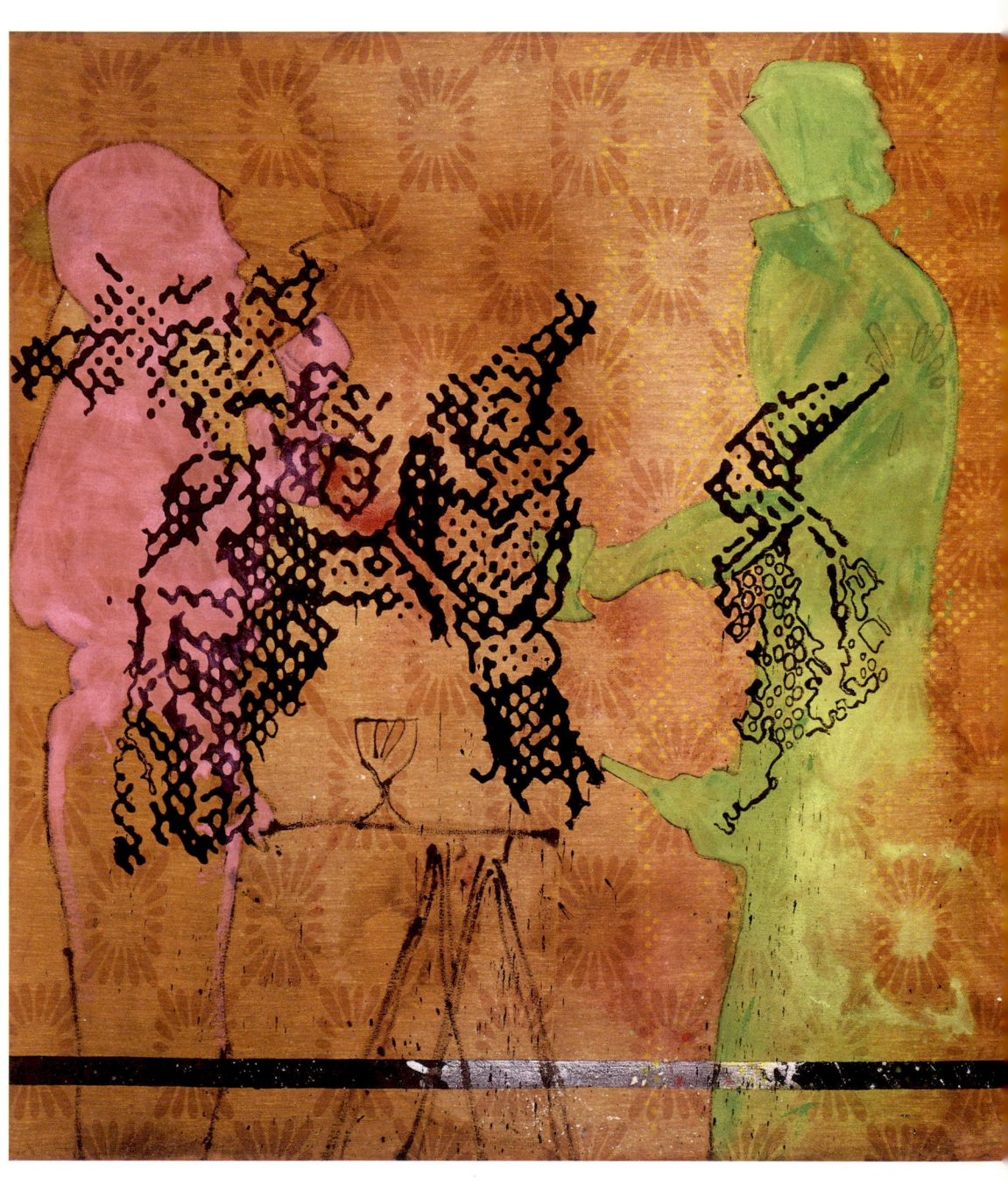

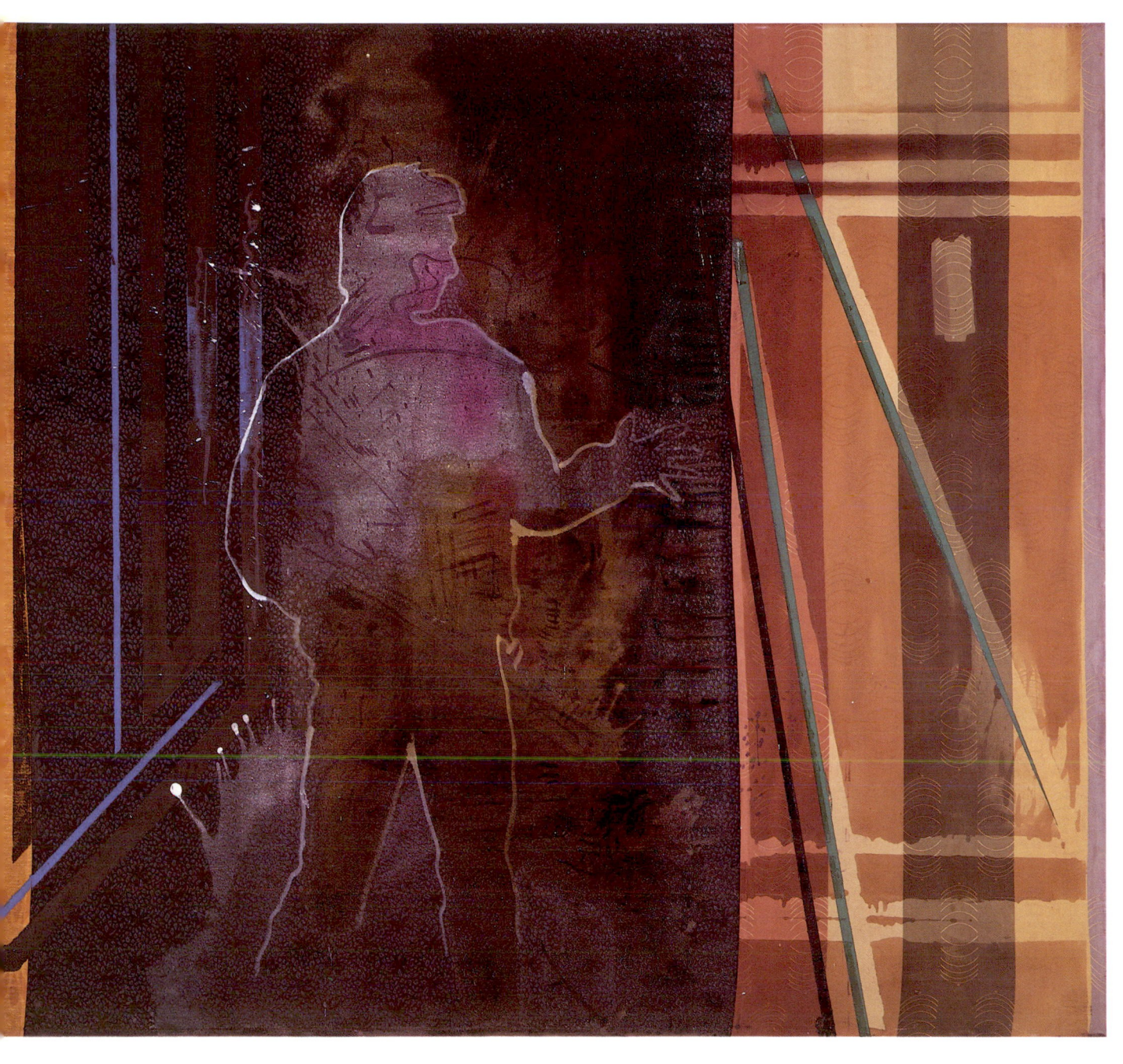

43. *Georg and Gugu* 1983

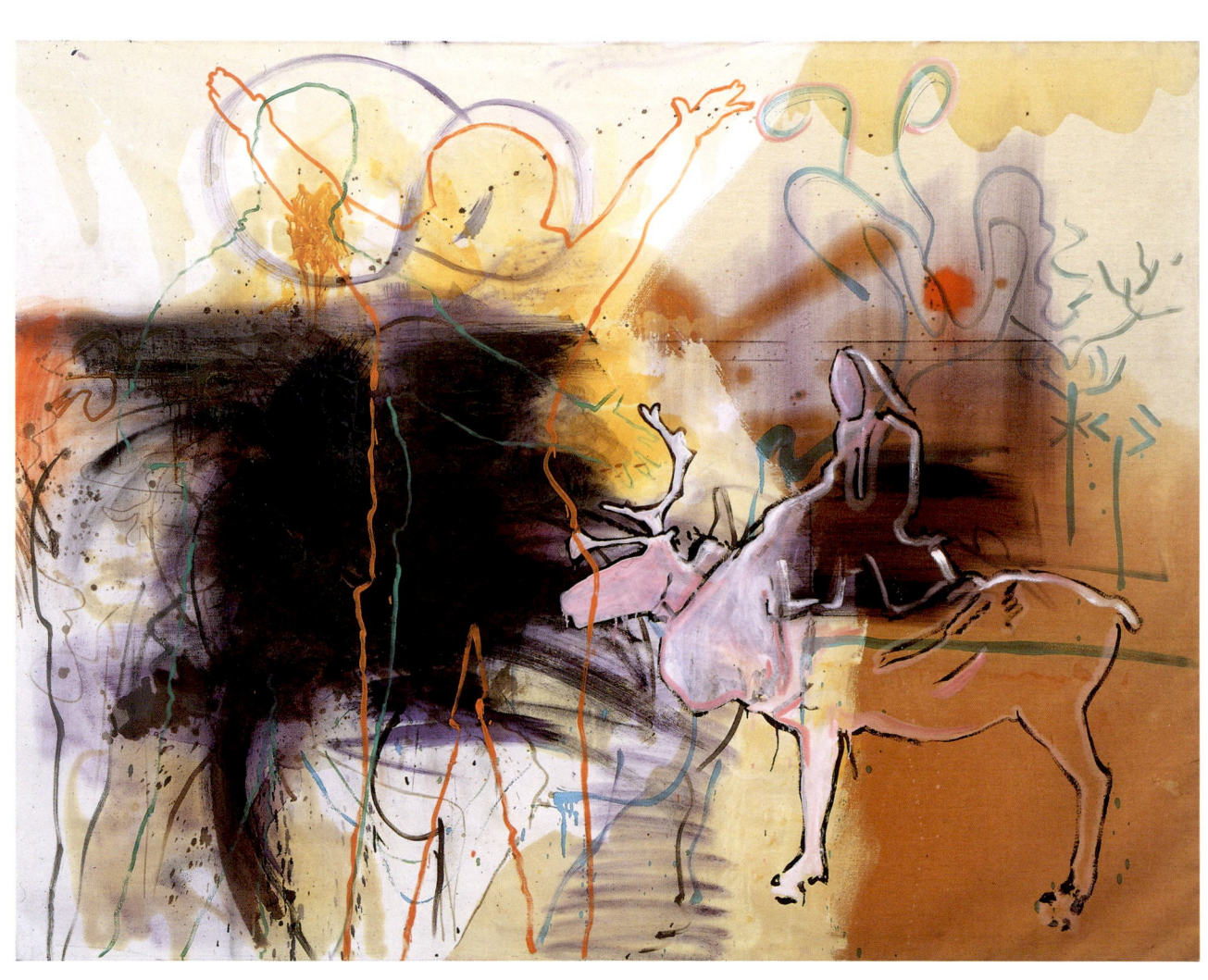

44. *Lapland Journey I* 1984

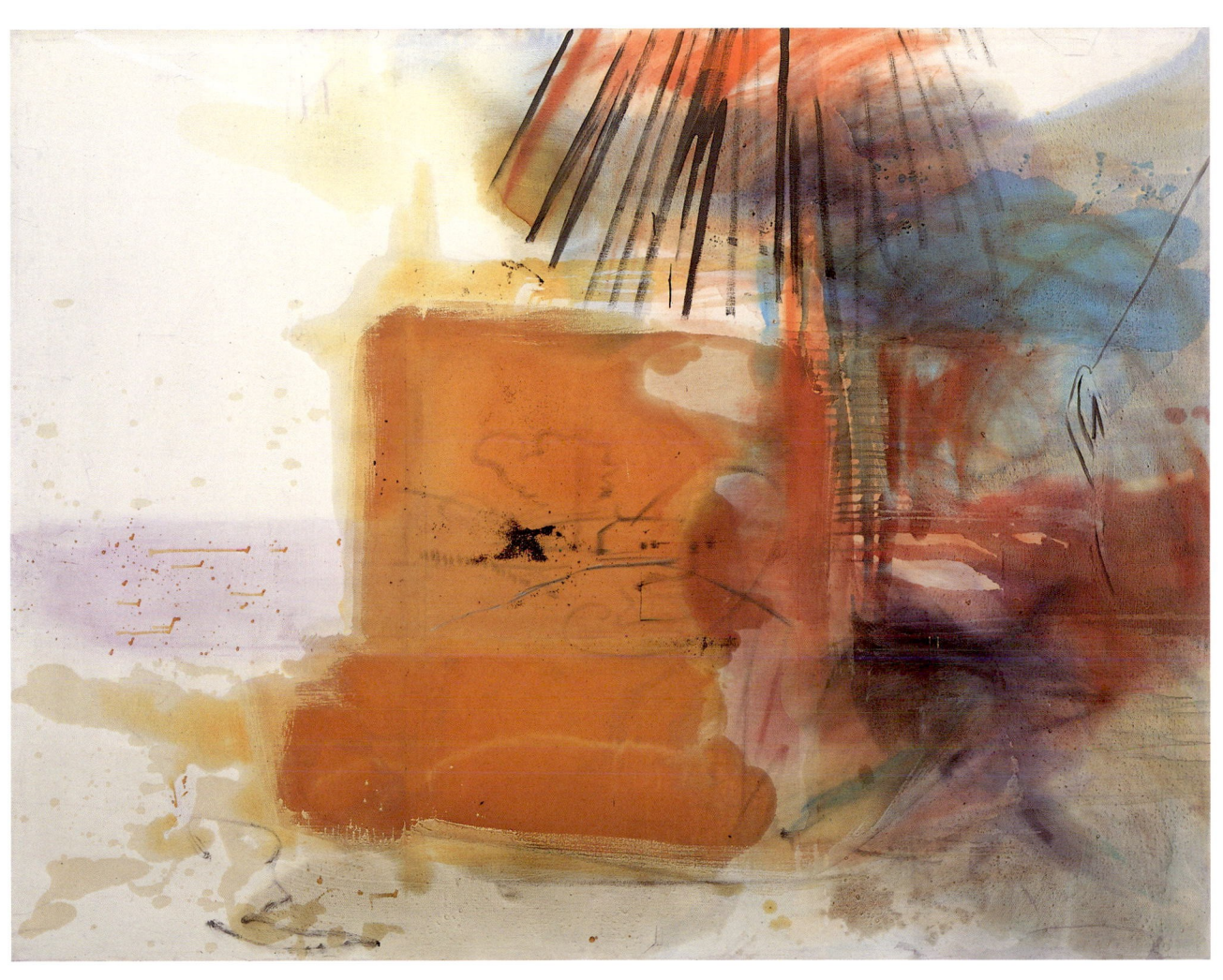

45. *Lapland Journey II* 1984

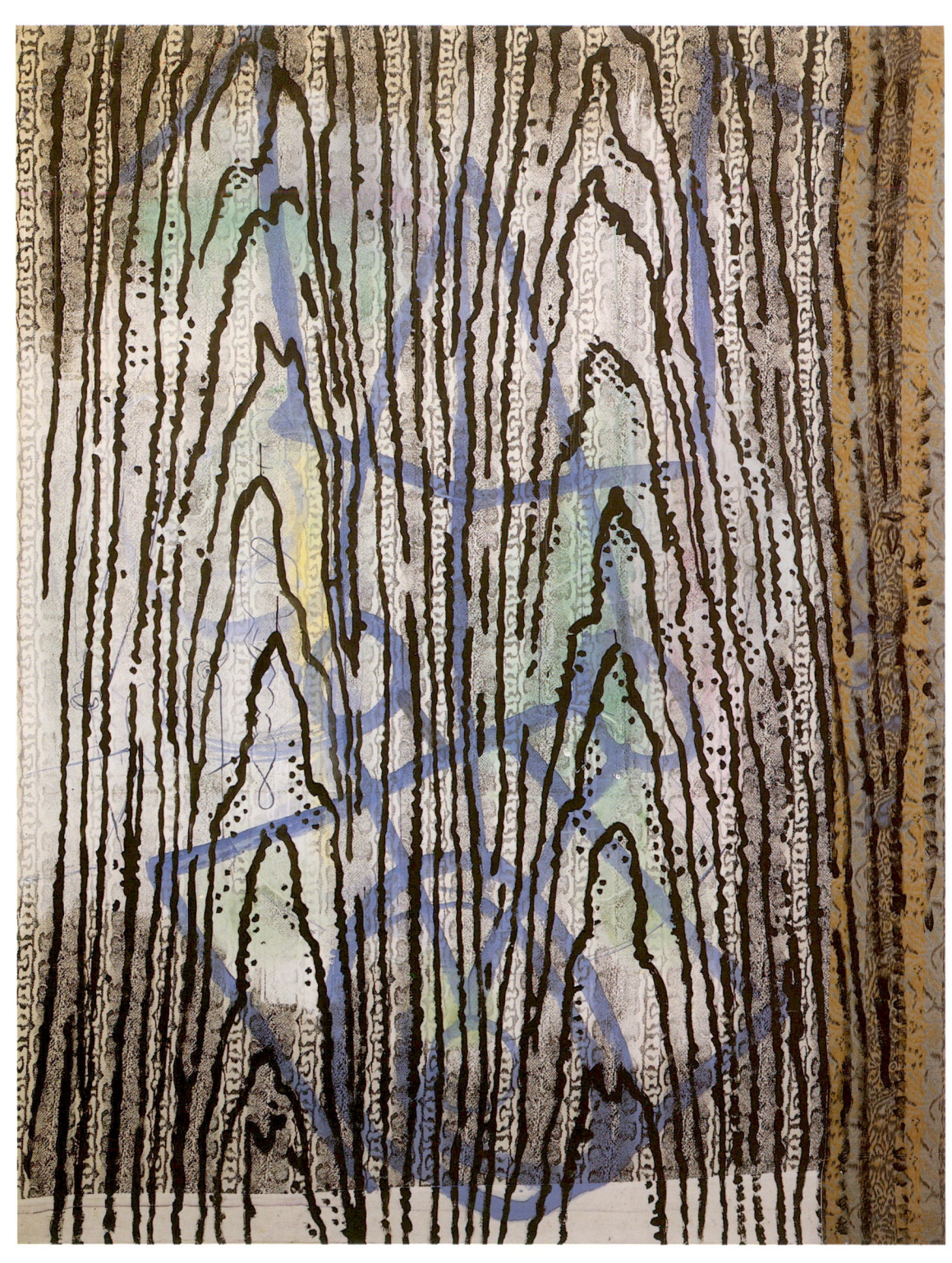

46. *Lapland Journey III (Adoration of the Kings: before Leonardo)* 1984

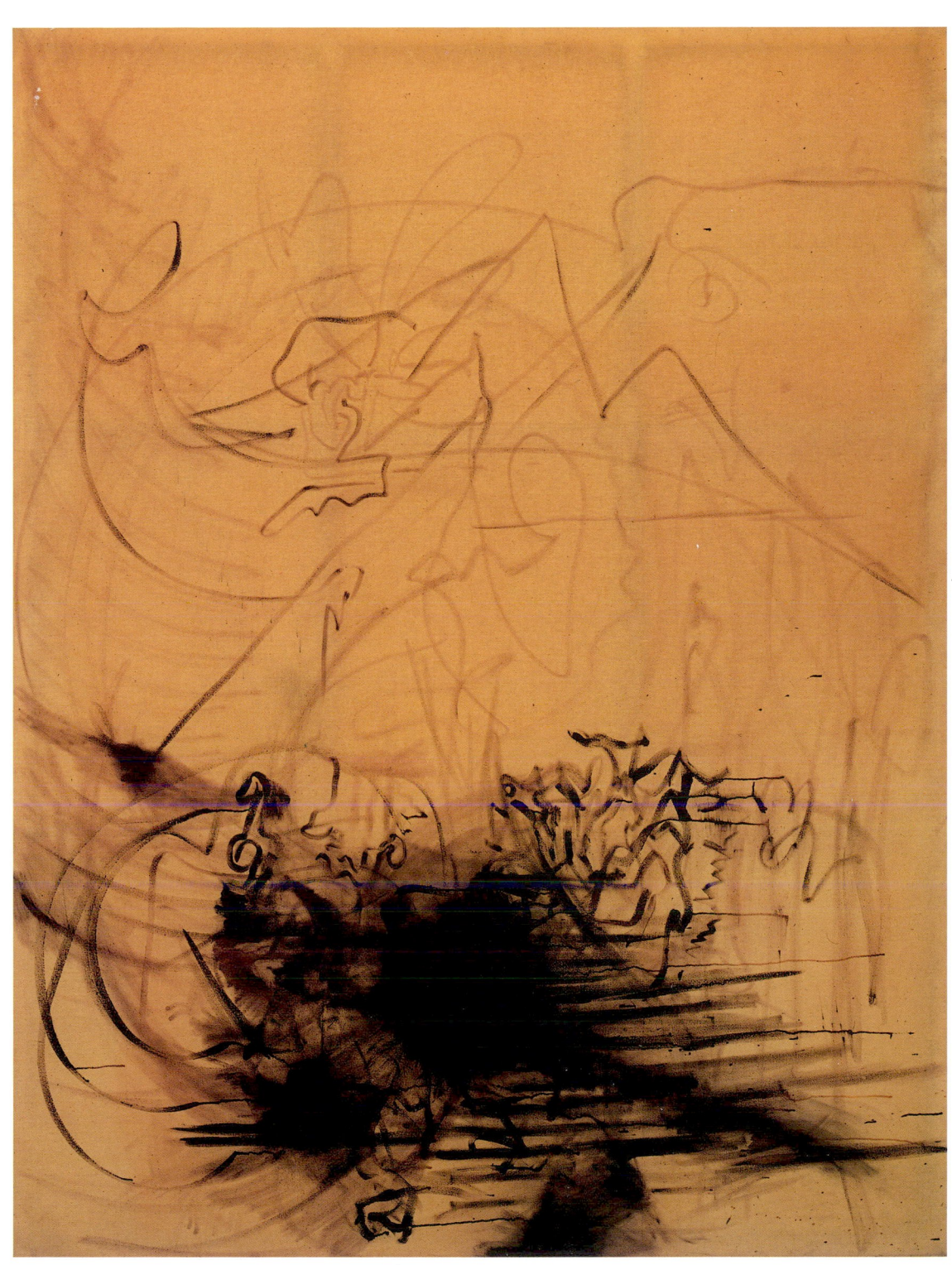

47. *Lapland Journey IV (Adoration of the Kings: after Leonardo)* 1984

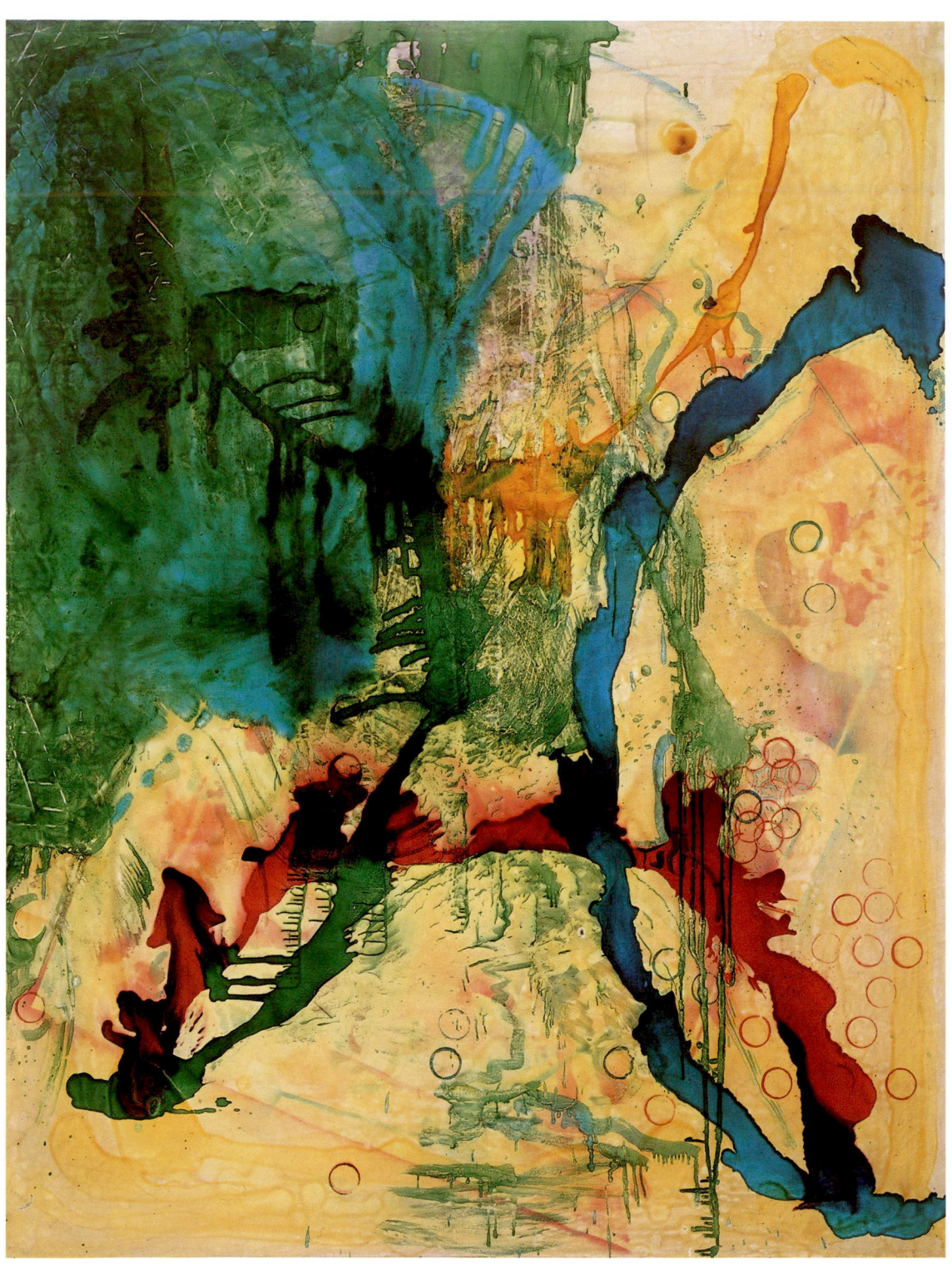

48. *Lapland Journey V (Leonardo)* 1984

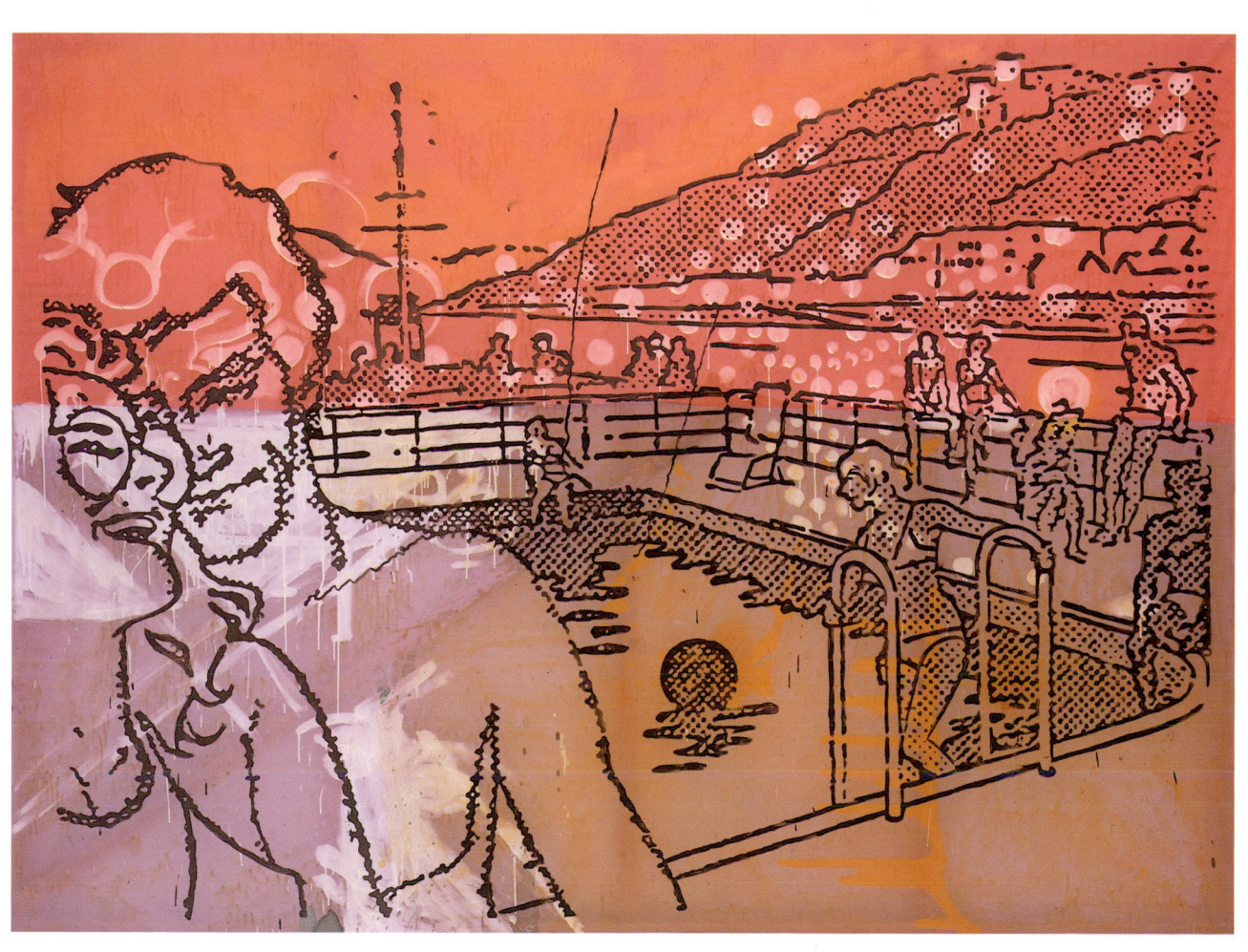

50. *Swimming Pool* 1988

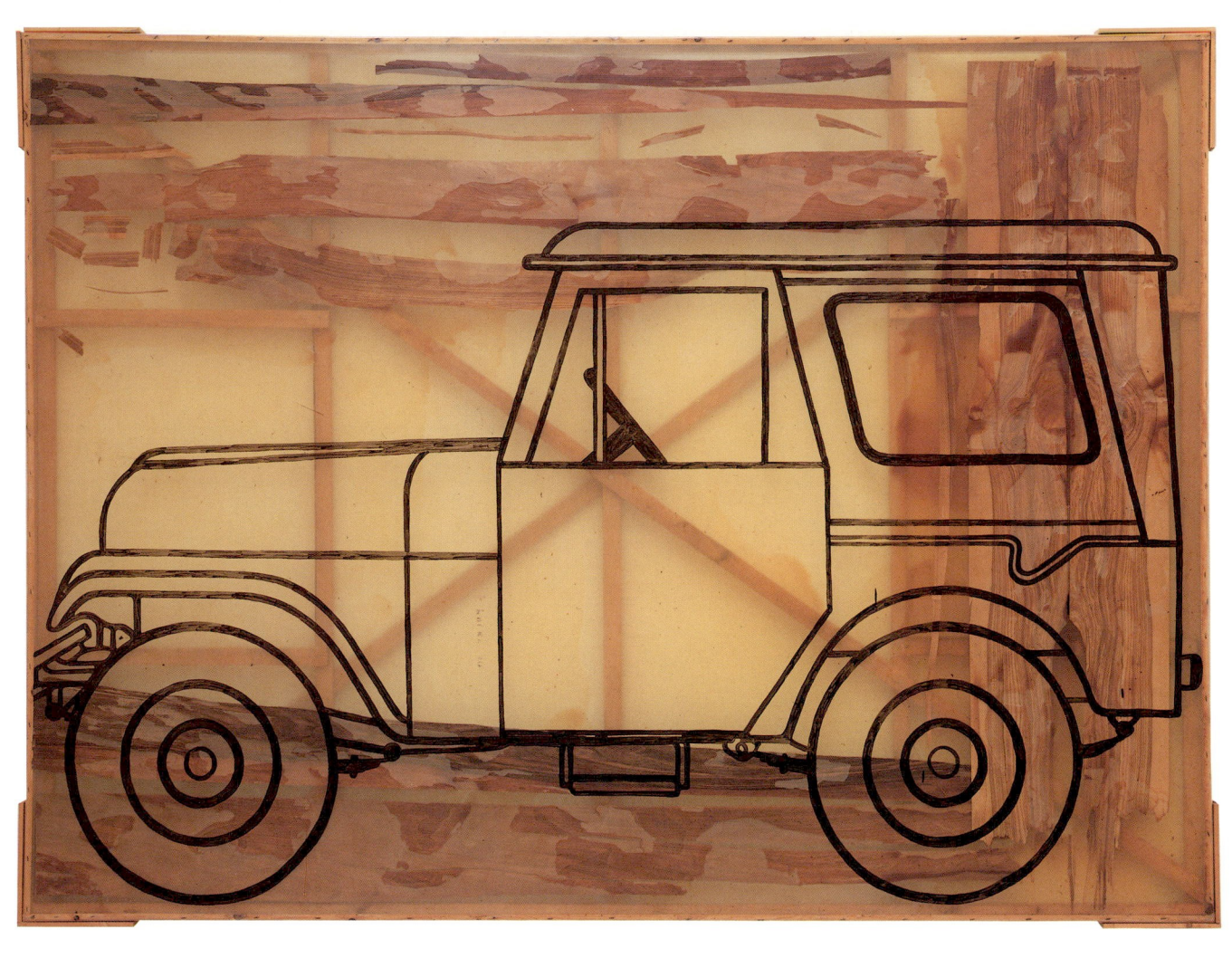

58. *Jeep* 1994

Sigmar Polke: betrayed lover

Thomas McEvilley

A great deal has been written about Sigmar Polke and his work, and as these writings multiply, a consensus seems to be taking shape. Several recent essays seem more or less to agree on the actual significance of Polke's notoriously ambiguous oeuvre. Kevin Power calls Polke 'possibly the most significant artist in the latter part of this century', then explains why. Polke, he says, 'surrender[s] himself to the surprise of process'. If there is a 'common denominator in his wide range of work', it may be its 'resistance to being appropriated at any single level of meaning', because Polke 'delights in cultivated contradictions'.[1] His work is inherently subversive, like 'anarchic sniping', 'bringing everything into a zone of doubt, putting all under erasure, wilfully mis-reading'.[2]

Donald Kuspit seems more or less to agree when he describes Polke's work as 'the pursuit of unintelligibility'. There is something 'nihilistic' in this pursuit, he says, since if art succeeds in being unintelligible it will 'do away with itself'. 'If art is really to be inarticulate, it is not art; it is suicidal for it to pursue the unintelligible'.[3]

Paul Groot seems pointed in the same direction when he focuses on 'how easily ... Polke can distance himself from the official story', because he is always 'fleeing from his own past', from a 'fear of being fixed into clichés'. He runs away 'from his own shadow' and becomes, as artist, 'a shadowy consciously created double'[4] of himself. The critic aiming at his work, then, can never hit it, because of his artful dodging: he is not there, only this shadowy double who signs his work.

Finally, to mention just one more of several possible instances, Prudence Carlson describes Polke as, 'shunning the snares of sharp identity', as he makes 'an art out of proclivities at once contradictory and enigmatical, scathing and perverse'. His work is 'governed by unbounded scepticism', and 'finds veracity only in the suspension of all systems of belief'.[5]

These related opinions are based not only on statements made in interviews by the artist himself, but also on an observation of the apparently contradictory confluences of visual elements in the work. Benday dots combined with organic abstraction; images from history with unstable chemicals thrown over them; images from prehistory alongside images from popular culture – the amalgamation of such elements in one inwardly contradictory canvas, such as the masterwork *Paganini* 1981–3 (p18), suggests an impulse to undermine the inherited Western traditions of the pictorial process.

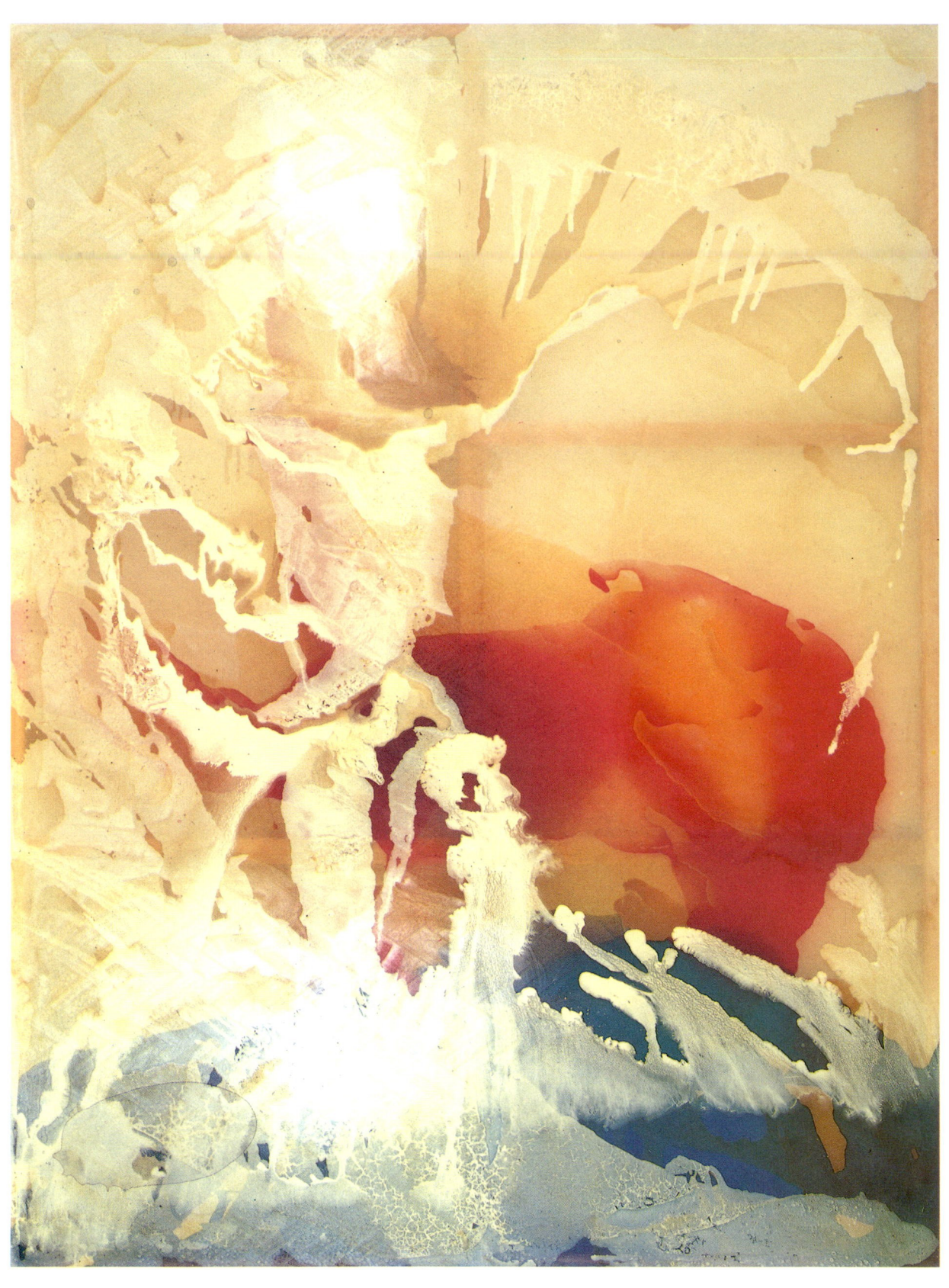

Apparition I 1992 (triptych), artificial resin, lacquer on fabric, Private Collection

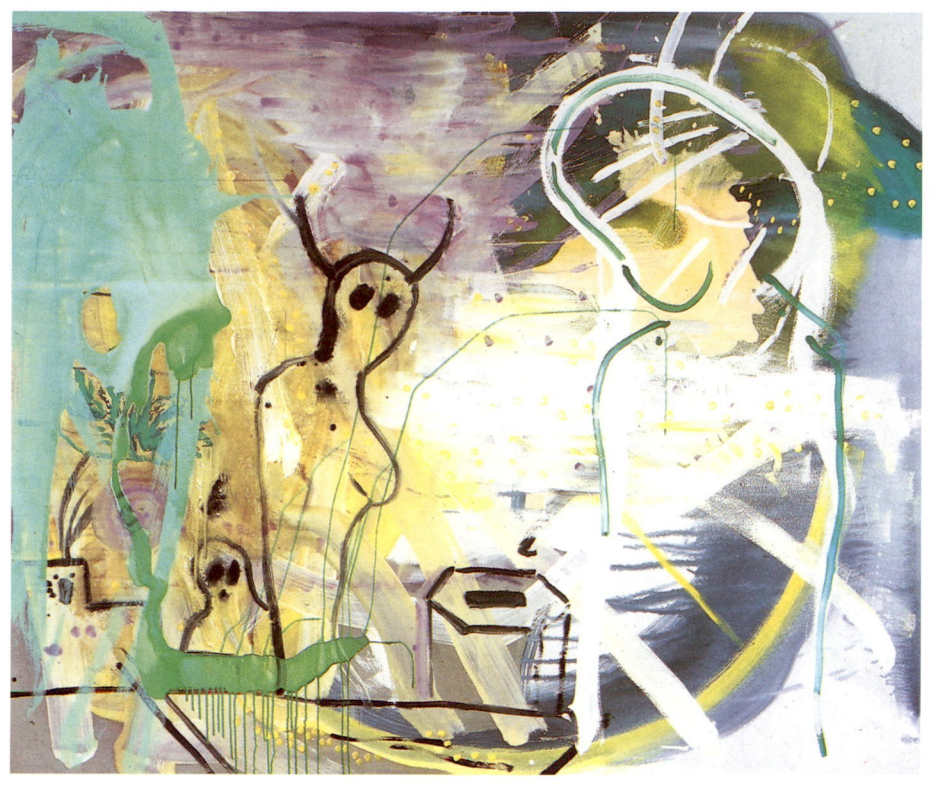

37. *Ghost* 1982

All that clearly seems true, and to be a reading that the works themselves are very deliberately proposing or inviting. The funny thing is that, if Polke is so unintelligible and such a universally sceptical dodger of meanings, then how come there's this complete and ultimately easy consensus about him? Isn't there a contradiction here? The clarity with which the critics see the stance of his work suggests that he is not, for all his vaunted scepticism, acting insincerely. He is being perfectly earnest and committed in his stance.

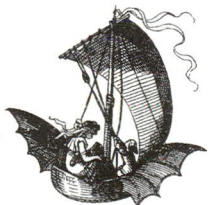

This portrayal of Polke as a continually changing sceptical de-constructivist seems to me to overlook certain qualities of the oeuvre, for example, its thematic integrity and stylistic wholeness. Both of these traits are characteristic of classical Modernism, an ideological construction of the pictorial which Polke has stringently renounced. Of course it is true that one of the fascinations of Polke's work is how different various pictures look from one another. Compare, for example, *Jeep* (p80) and *Apparition I* (p82), both from 1992, but both very different, seeming to assume radically different ideas of pictorial integrity. What I am pointing to is not the use of multiple styles, but the fact that the various styles are consistently strong and, as it were, frontal in their depictions. There is a consistency of sensibility lurking behind them, more so, perhaps, than in the oeuvre of his peer Gerhard Richter.

Polke has expressed his aim, at least in part, as the deconstruction of Modernist ideas of the sacredness and integrity of the artwork.[6] His betrayal of style is evidently intended as a betrayal of Modernism. Modernism was based on the idea of universals, and that meant that art and artists had to appear to be reflecting universals. Since universals don't change, the understanding was that artistic practice, or style, couldn't change either. (By remaining devoted to a signature style, an artist like Piet Mondrian, Barnett Newman, or Jackson Pollock demonstrated his allegiance to the universals as his sensibility received them.) On the contrary, Polke, by deliberately flaunting style, capriciously switching styles, or using styles as signifiers in the sense in which brushstrokes used to be, is understood to be demonstrating his disdain for Modernist universals and the hold they once exercised on artistic practice. This mobile approach to style, or to styles, adopting and then abandoning them for specific purposes, is a standard late Modernist and post-Modernist practice, found in the oeuvres of artists from Marcel Broodthaers to Dennis Oppenheim.[7]

But is the problem of style so easy to circumvent? Has Polke, not to mention these other artists, really gone beyond style, or has he simply rendered it more hidden and variable? Isn't there enough aesthetic and thematic coherence in Polke's oeuvre for it to be regarded as a style rather than a non-style? Isn't there a polished style of studied contradiction and artfully planted cross-currents? And isn't such a trait indeed typical of high and late Modernisms, as in oeuvres such as Francis Picabia's, Yves Klein's, and Piero Manzoni's?

I am not questioning the authenticity of Polke's stance as much as the distinction between Modernism and post-Modernism. Polke, who is regarded as one of the quintessentially post-Modernist artists, demonstrates, I believe, a consistent commitment to a position and a style – even though that style is characterised by the appearance (or the pretence?) of negating style.

This situation raises the question of whether so-called post-Modernism might simply be a disguised manifestation of late Modernism. Polke's apparent inability to get beyond the problem of style would seem to imply this. Indeed, most self-consciously post-Modernist artists seem to me to have at least one foot in Modernism.[8] Polke's stance is ironic yet intense; its irony is, in a sense, undercut by its earnest intensity. Like so much of post-Modernist cultural manifestation, it barely conceals a puritanical desire to preserve Modernism or at least some parts of it, precisely by critiquing it and bringing it back to health.

The question still facing post-Modern culture is whether to preserve, reject or

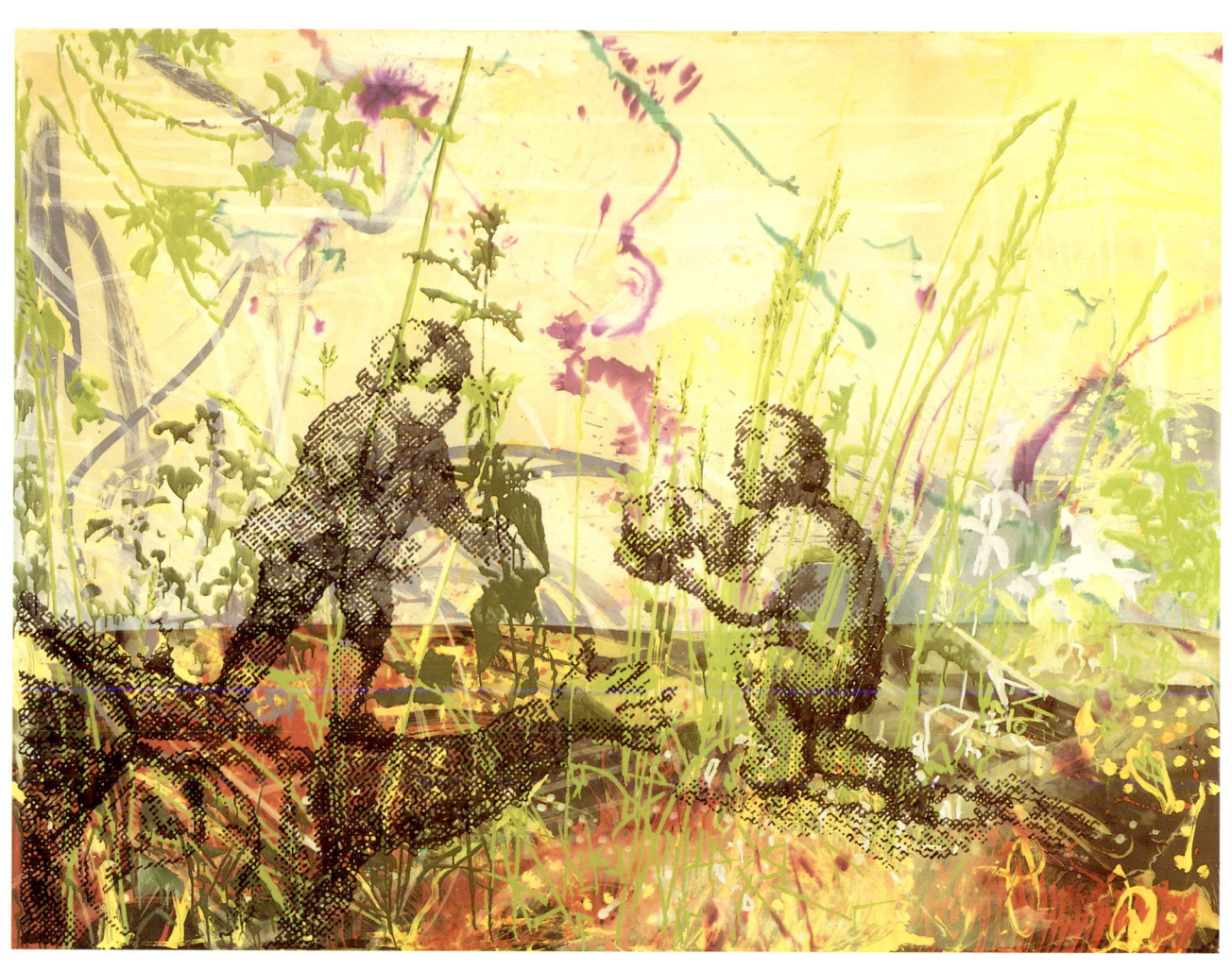

51. *Children's Games* (Jeux d'enfants) 1988

modify the package of bourgeois democratic ideals as it was first clearly enunciated in the funeral oration of Pericles, in the second book of Thucydides's *History*. This package of ideas involved bourgeois individualism, democratic constitutions, reason as a means to social engineering, scepticism about religion and tradition, and governmental socialism. Revived some 2,400 years later in the work of British, French and German philosophers, these ideas became known as the Enlightenment. They were essential elements of Modernism.

When Modernism lost credibility in the 1960s and 1970s, there were two new options which arose: pre-Modern revivalism, whereby cultural connections with ancient, supposedly pre-patriarchal societies, were to be re-opened, and post-Modern revisionism, wherein Modernism was not to be entirely rejected but revised methodologically, in the hope of a saner future. Polke's work, in its early phases, often tilted toward pre-Modern revivalism,[9] in the works, for example, devoted to Native American realities. More recently it has seemed to focus on the option of post-Modern revisionism. The works involving the French Revolution, such as *Children's Games* 1988 (p85), and the Stalinist period of Eastern European culture, such as the *Watchtower* series of 1984 and after, unmistakably focus on issues of Modernism, its disasters, and its dreams. These works are critical of Modernism, but they do not straightforwardly reject it. They seem to me to exude a certain nostalgia for Enlightenment ideals and a sense that those ideals are still viable foundations for civilised thought.

There is a sorrow in Polke's works about Modernism, such as *Le jour de gloire est arrivé* 1988, which shows the dead of the French Revolution scattered about the staircase of history; the blobby presence of natural chemicals overlays their cultural intensity as if they were, say, insects. But this is a sorrow not as of something which utterly failed, so much as of something that almost got there but somehow got derailed. There is a lament for history and its disasters, its failure as an idea and as a practice. Yet underneath this lament there seems to be a strong force toward belief. One laments for what one loved that went wrong, not for what one never loved. As Power accurately observes, Polke 'undermines as a means of advance'.[10] He still, in other words, has the traditional Modernist belief in progress, but believes that at present it is most likely to be advanced by deconstructing Modernism as a larger frame. If, as William Wilson says, art is *'a way of thinking about reality'*,[11] then Polke's oeuvre strikes me as double-edged. On the one hand it does clearly involve structures of conflict and contradiction which espouse or suggest a generally sceptical stance toward meaning; but on the other hand it shows a deep commitment to human life and its potential.

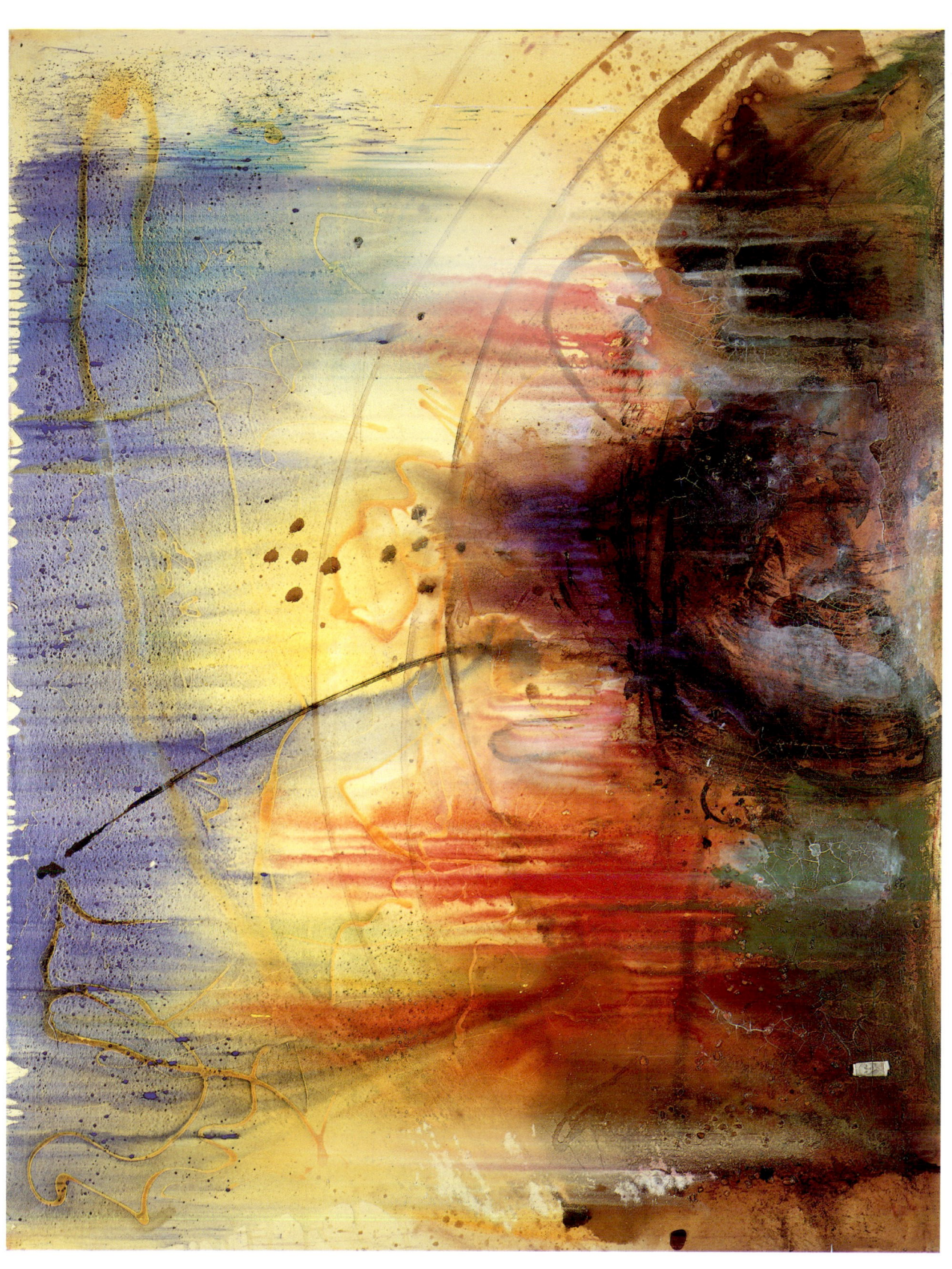

42. *Madam Tucher's Veil* 1983

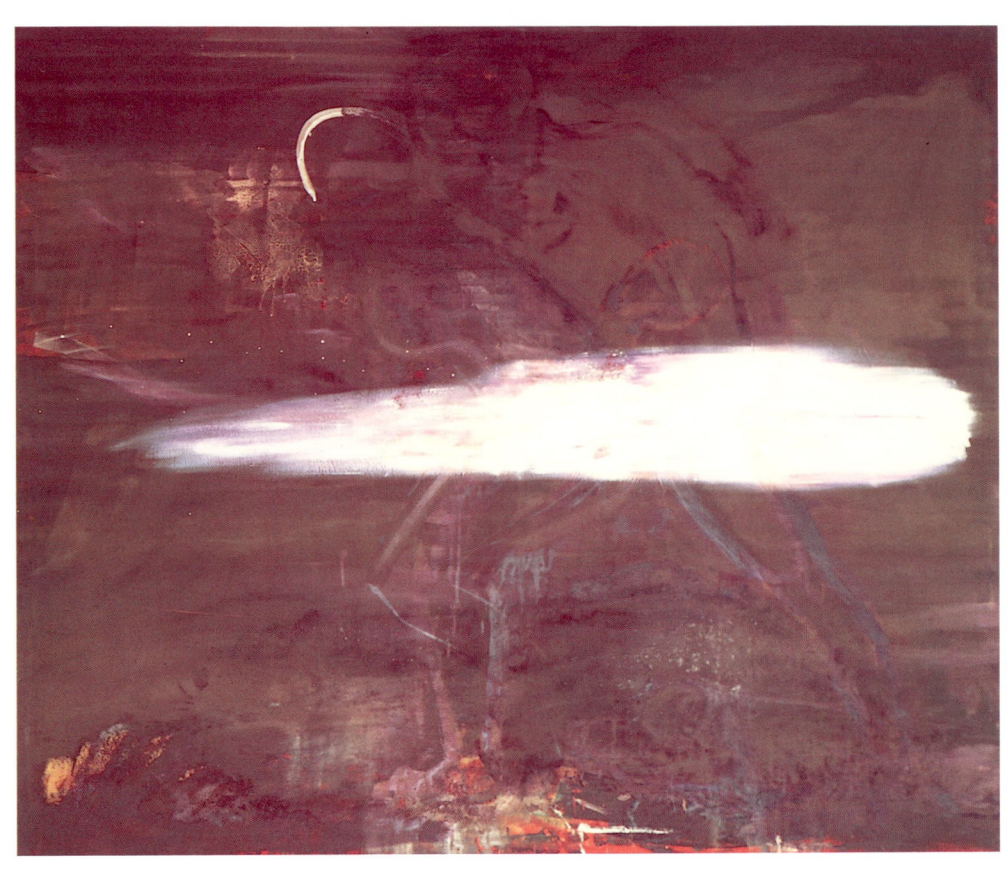

36. *Comet* 1982

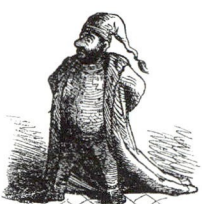

If Polke is to be seen as a late disappointed lover of Modernism, who felt betrayed by its excesses, does this substantially change the critical approach to his work? Or does it, more broadly, reveal, yet again, something that is hidden within the Modernism/post-Modernism debates? It has been suggested before that post-Modernism is more accurately to be regarded as a late revisionist phase of Modernism, an attempt to retain the Enlightenment package without the crypto-religious elements that seem to have turned that package vicious and rendered it harmful to the entire world. It might seem to be a thematic commitment of this type that gives Polke's oeuvre its Modernist sense of overall coherence.

It is of course true, that this coherence involves deliberate use of apparent contradiction as a stylistic device. That contradiction might be described as an ambivalence about the values of Modernism and post-Modernism. It takes the form of an interpenetrated gyre of love and cynicism, neither impulse cancelling the other but each, in the peculiar way of sublation, somehow strengthening the other through the opposite.

1.   Kevin Power, 'Sigmar Polke', *frieze*, no 4, April–May 1992, p25.
2.   Kevin Power, 'Sigmar Polke: Subverting Intent', *Sigmar Polke*, Valencia, 1994, pp115-6.
3.   Donald Kuspit, 'Sigmar Polke', *ArtForum*, February 1987, pp111-2.
4.   Paul Groot, 'Sigmar Polke: Impervious to Facile Interpretations, Polke Wants to Reinstate the Mystery of the Painting', *Flash Art*, May-June 1988, p66.
5.   Prudence Carlson, *Polke: Drawings from the 1960s*, David Nolan Gallery, New York: 1987, pp5-6.
6.   See, for example, Groot, op. cit., p66: 'You have to say things that are forbidden... no modern sort of sacred iconography'.
7.   For more detail on this point see Thomas McEvilley, 'Modernism, Anti-Modernism and Post-Modernism in the Work of Dennis Oppenheim', in *Dennis Oppenheim: And the Mind Grew Fingers*, New York, 1991.
8.   For more on this see Thomas McEvilley, 'The Case of Julian Schnabel', *Julian Schnabel: Paintings 1975-1986*, London, 1986, pp9-19.
9.   See Thomas McEvilley, 'Flower Power: Trying to Say the Obvious About Sigmar Polke', *Parkett*, 1991, no 30, pp32-41.
10.   Kevin Power, 'Sigmar Polke: Subverting Intent', ibid, p115.
11.   William S. Wilson III, 'Art Energy and Attention', in *The New Art: a critical anthology*, Gregory Battcock (ed), New York, 1966

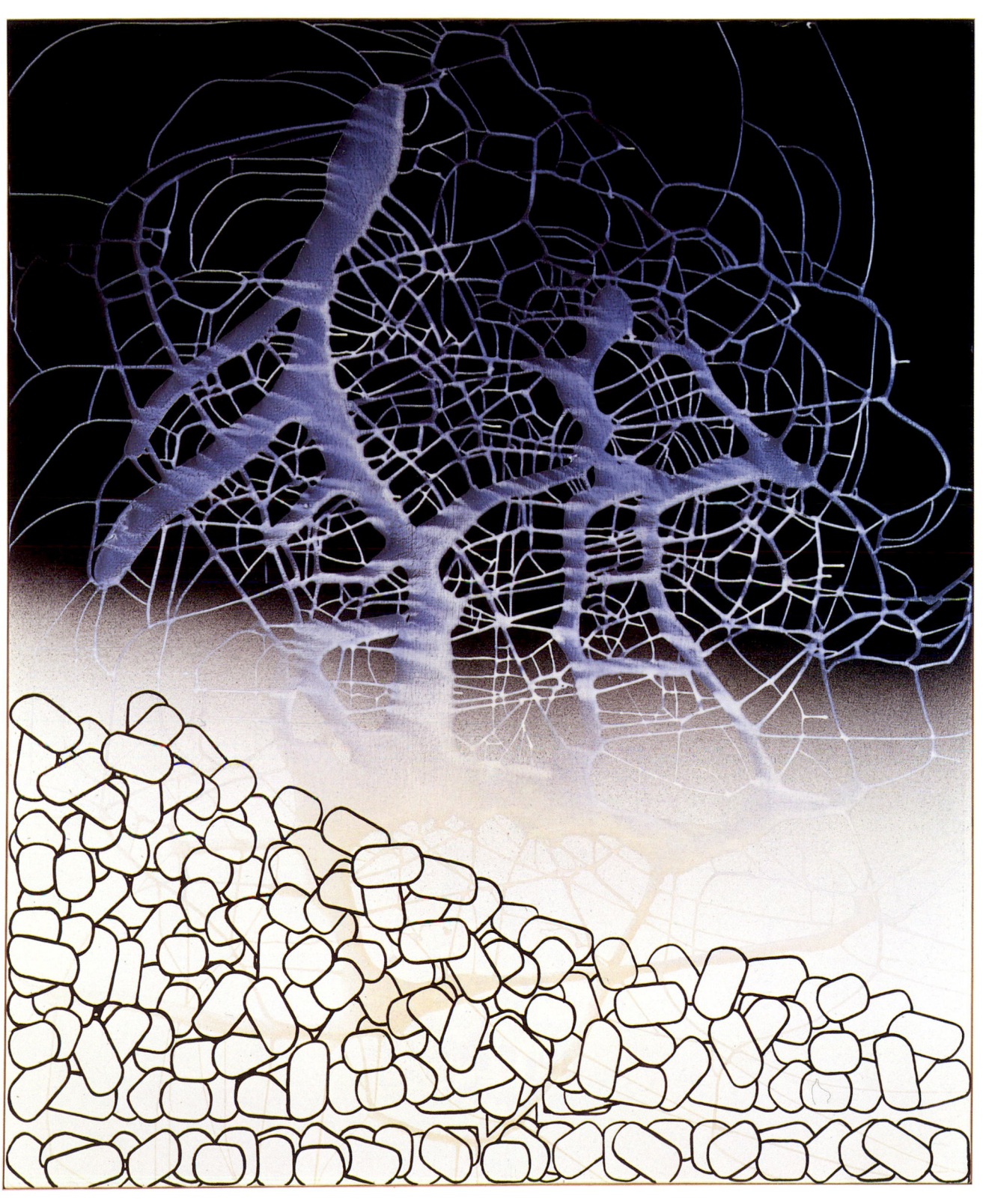

60. *Shrapnel* 1994

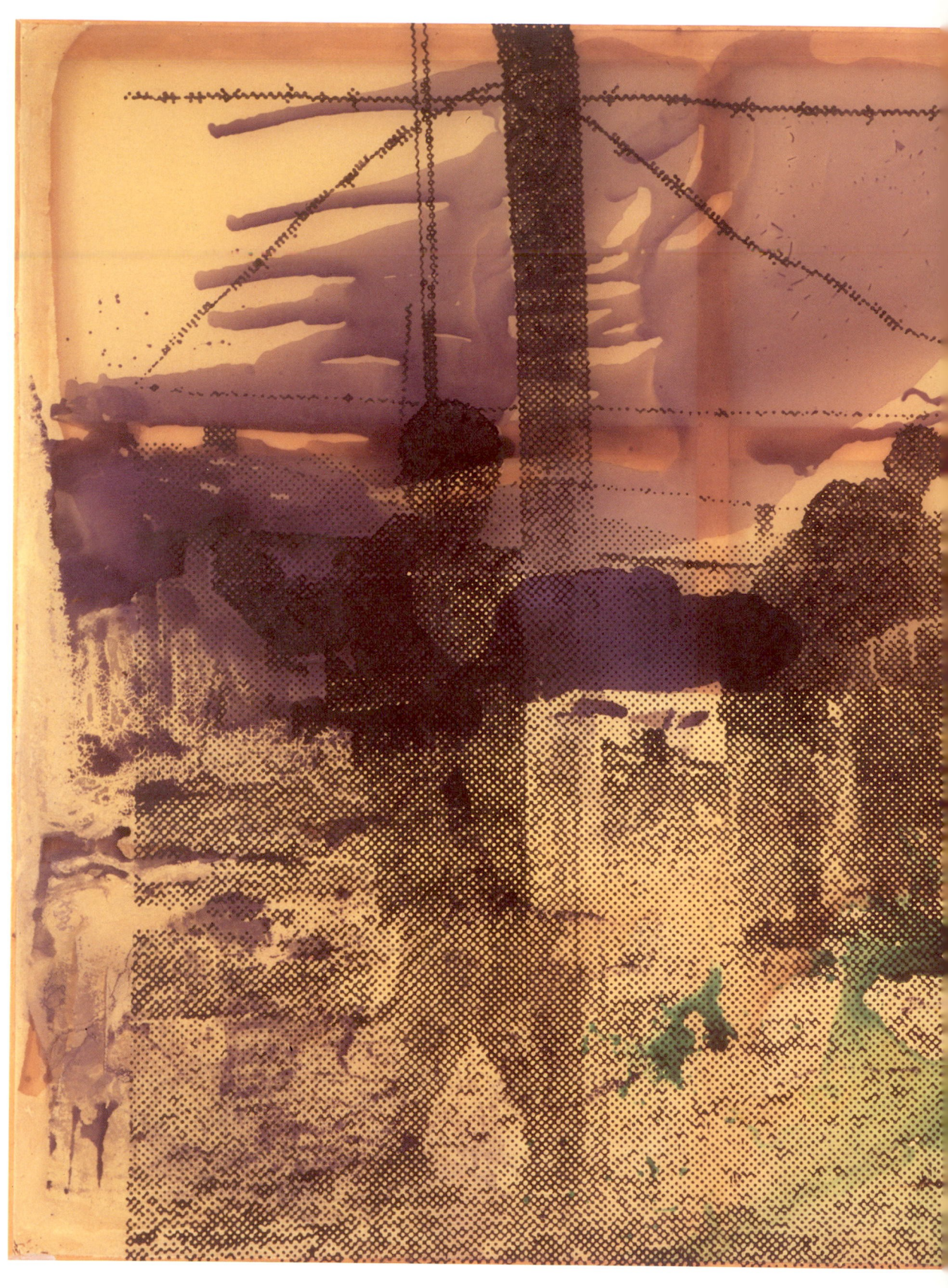

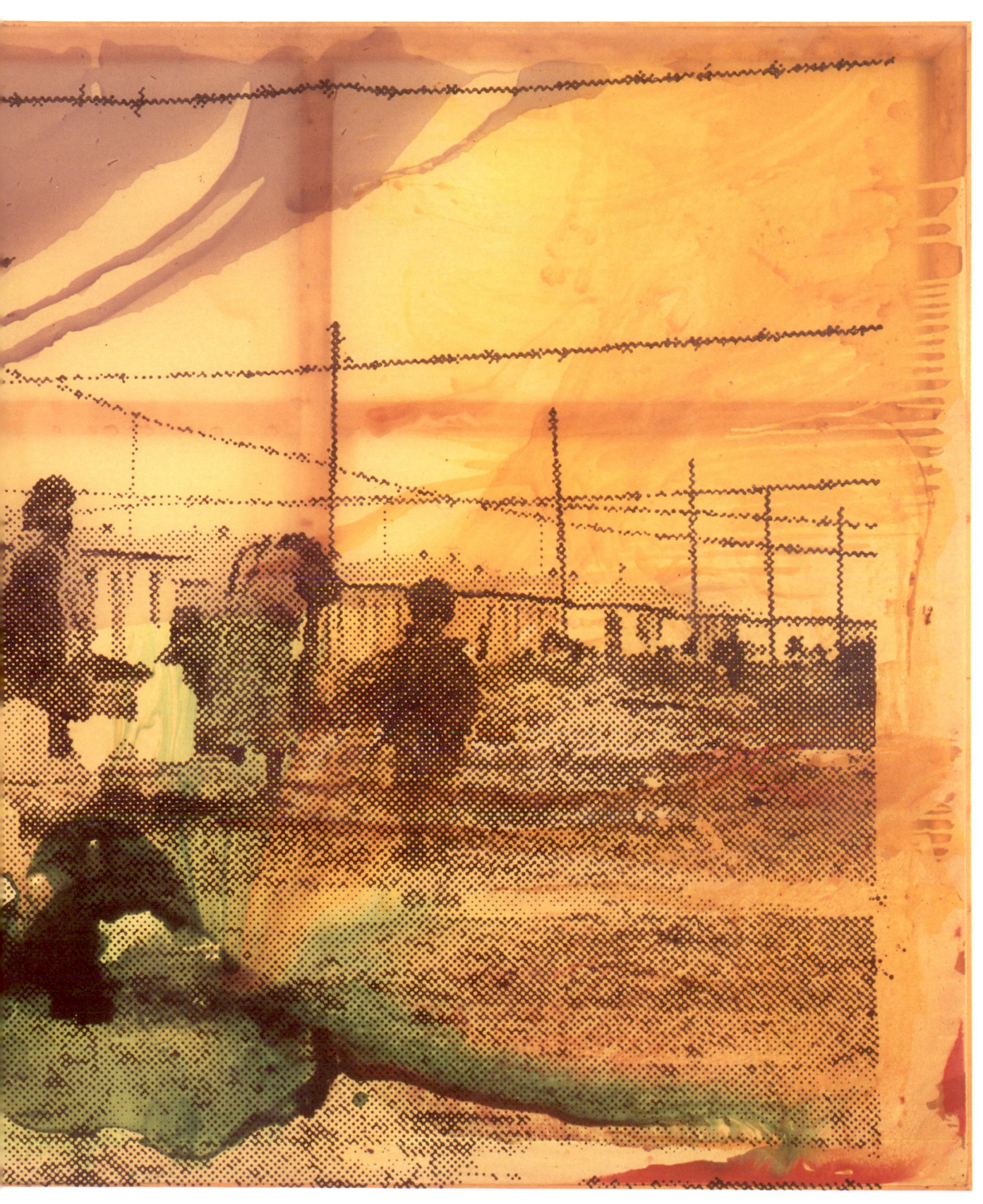

59. *Refugee Camp* 1994

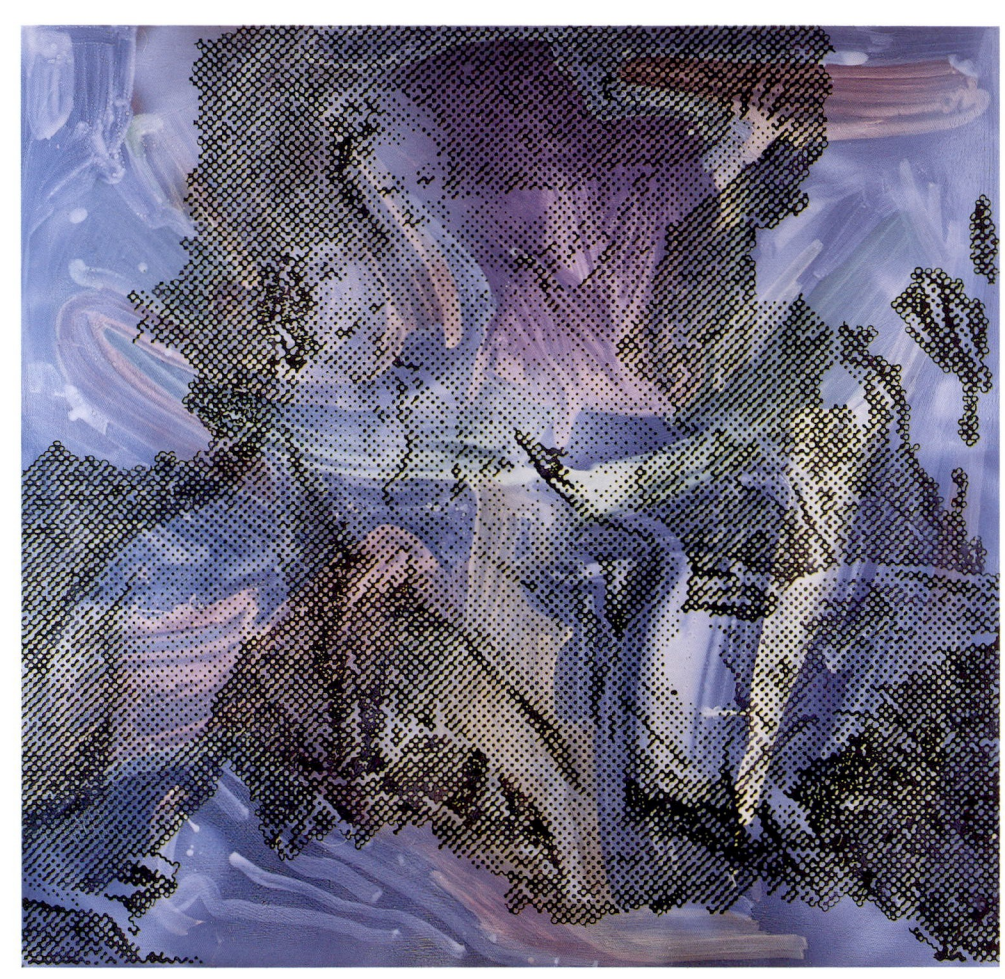

61. *Blue Boucher* 1994

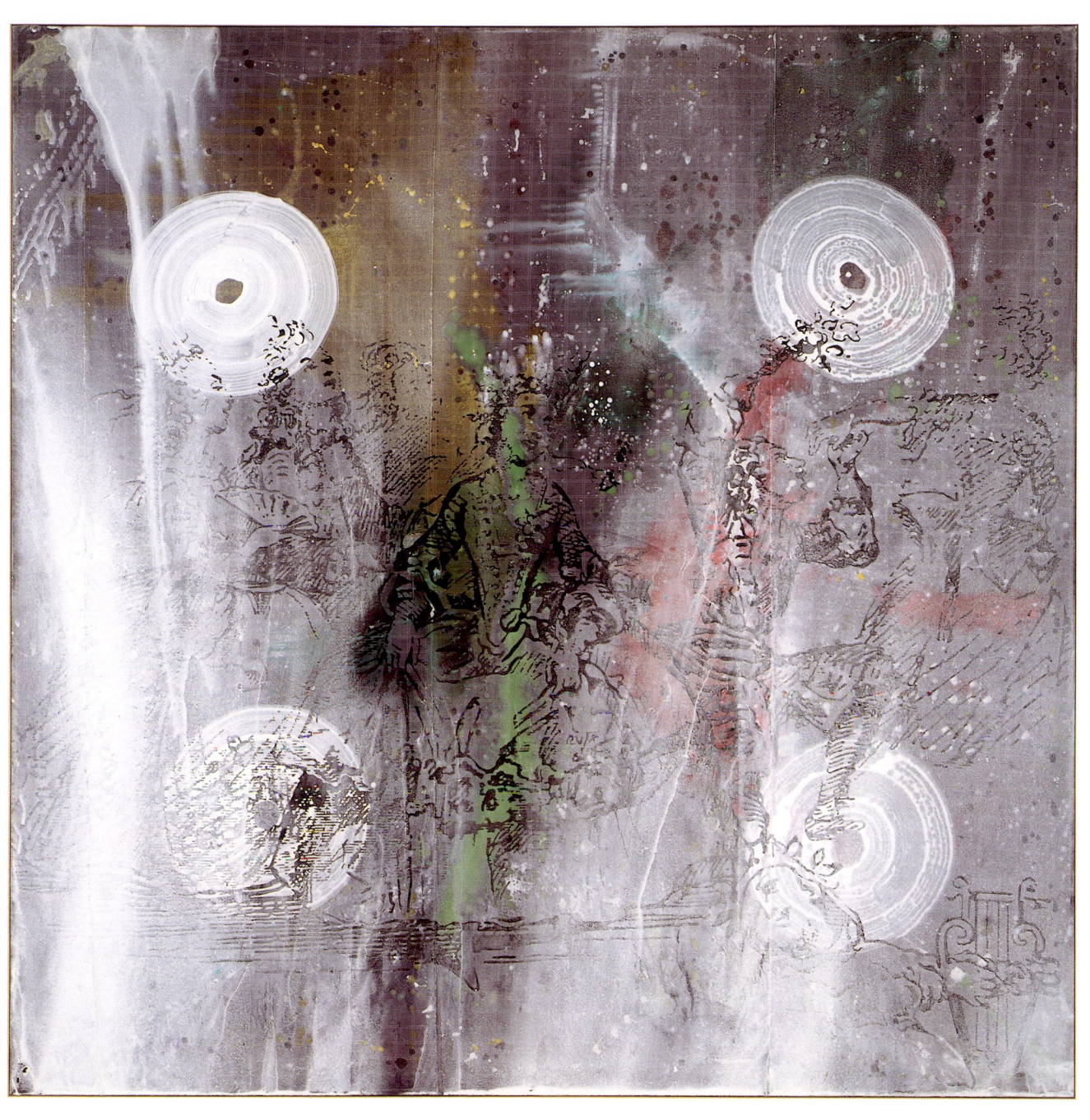

54. *Roccoco* 1994

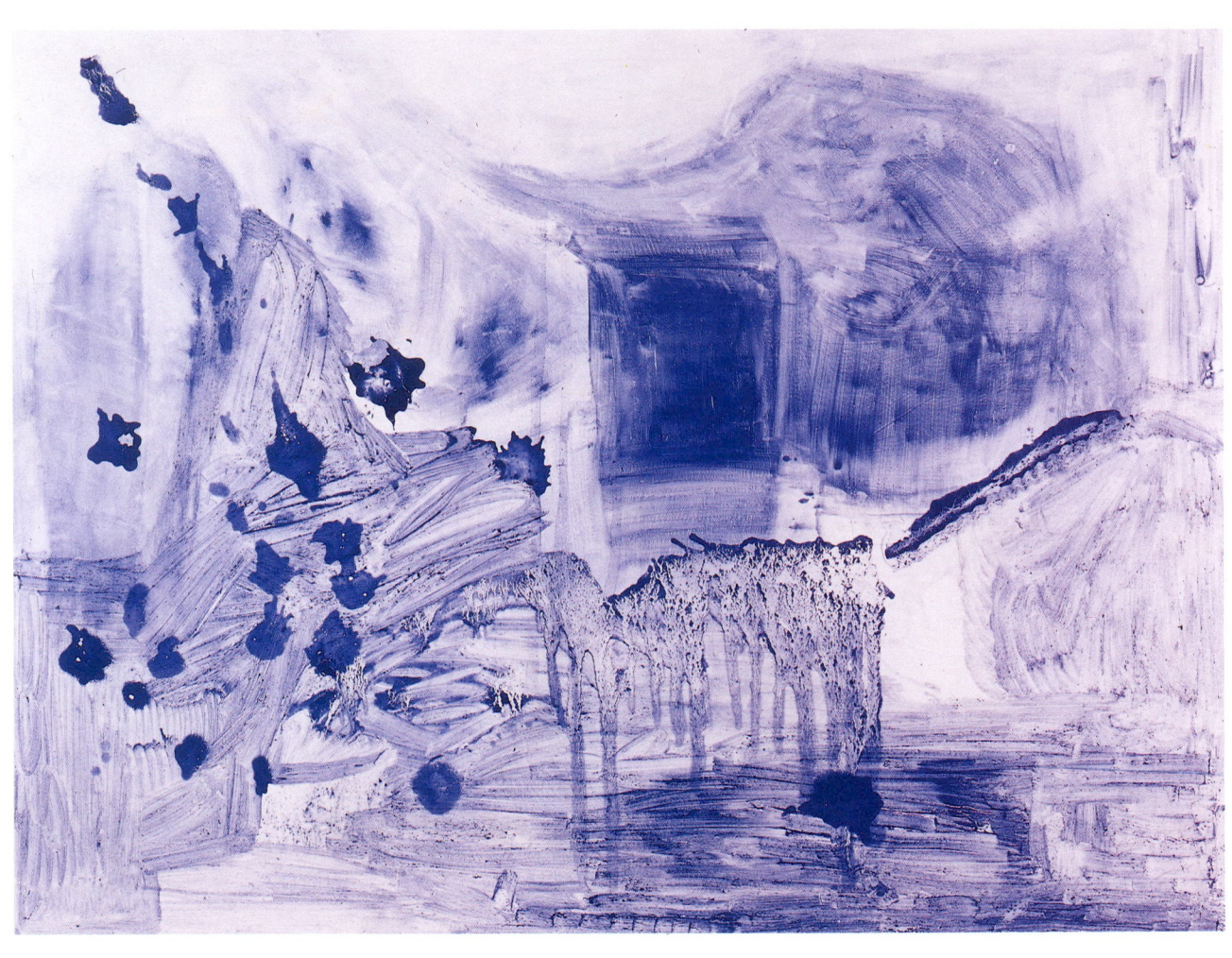

55. *Lapis Lazuli I* 1994

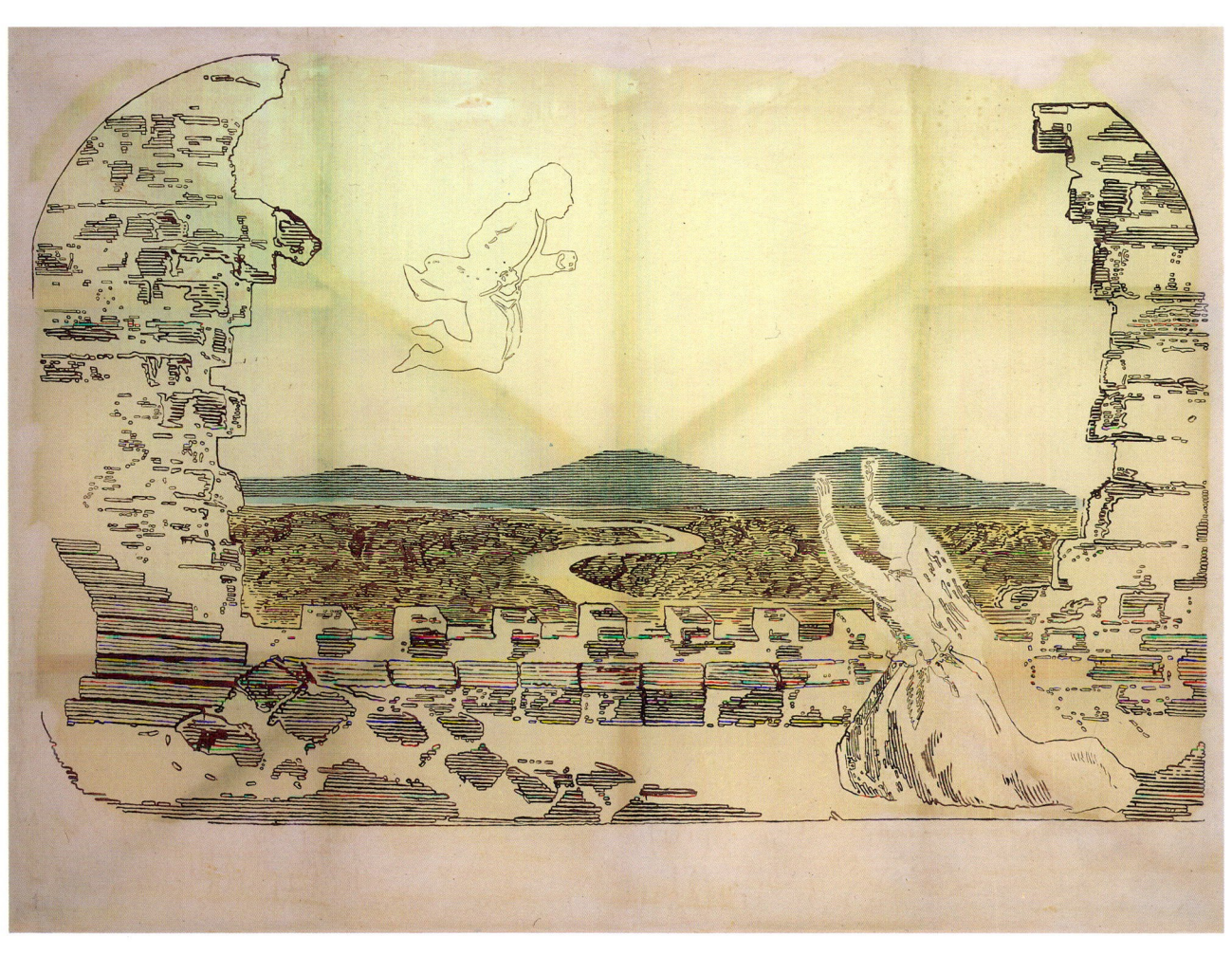

52. *Annunciation* 1992

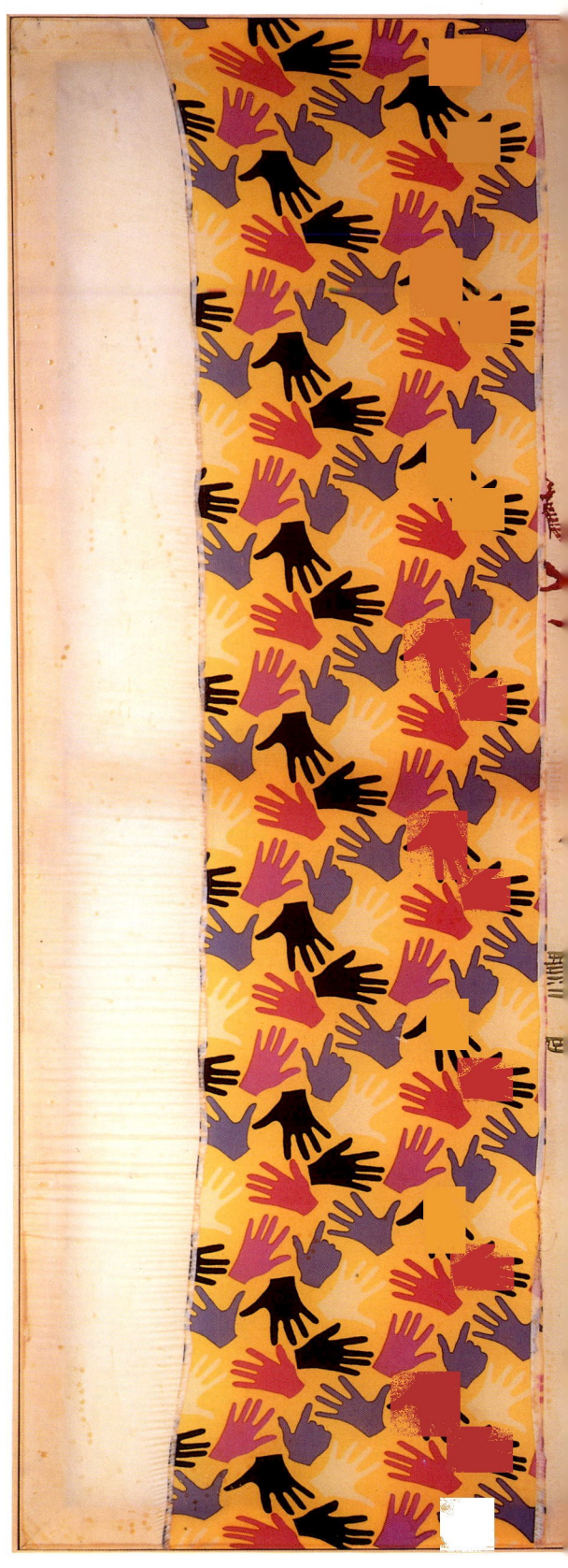

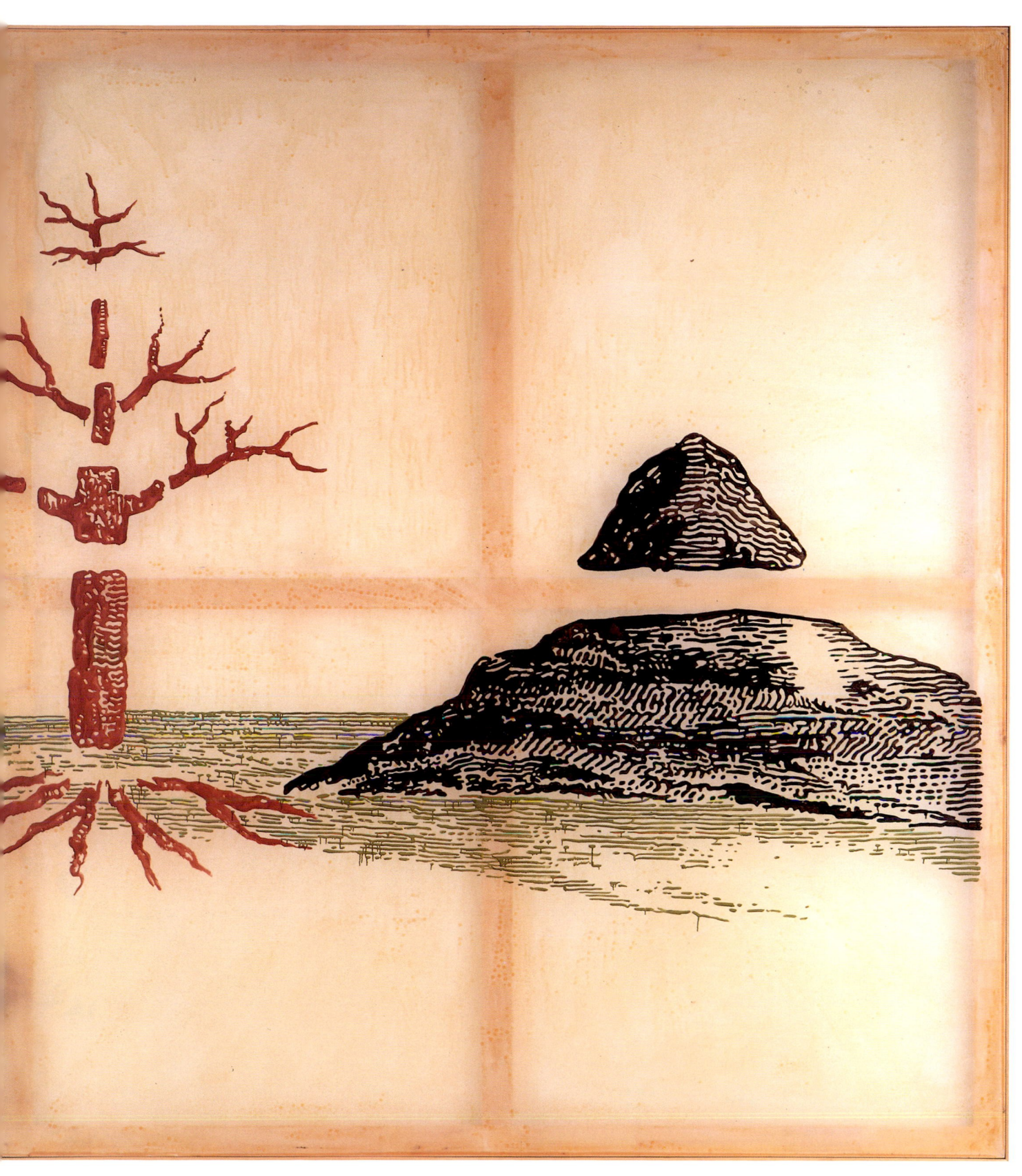

57. *The Three Lies of Painting* 1994

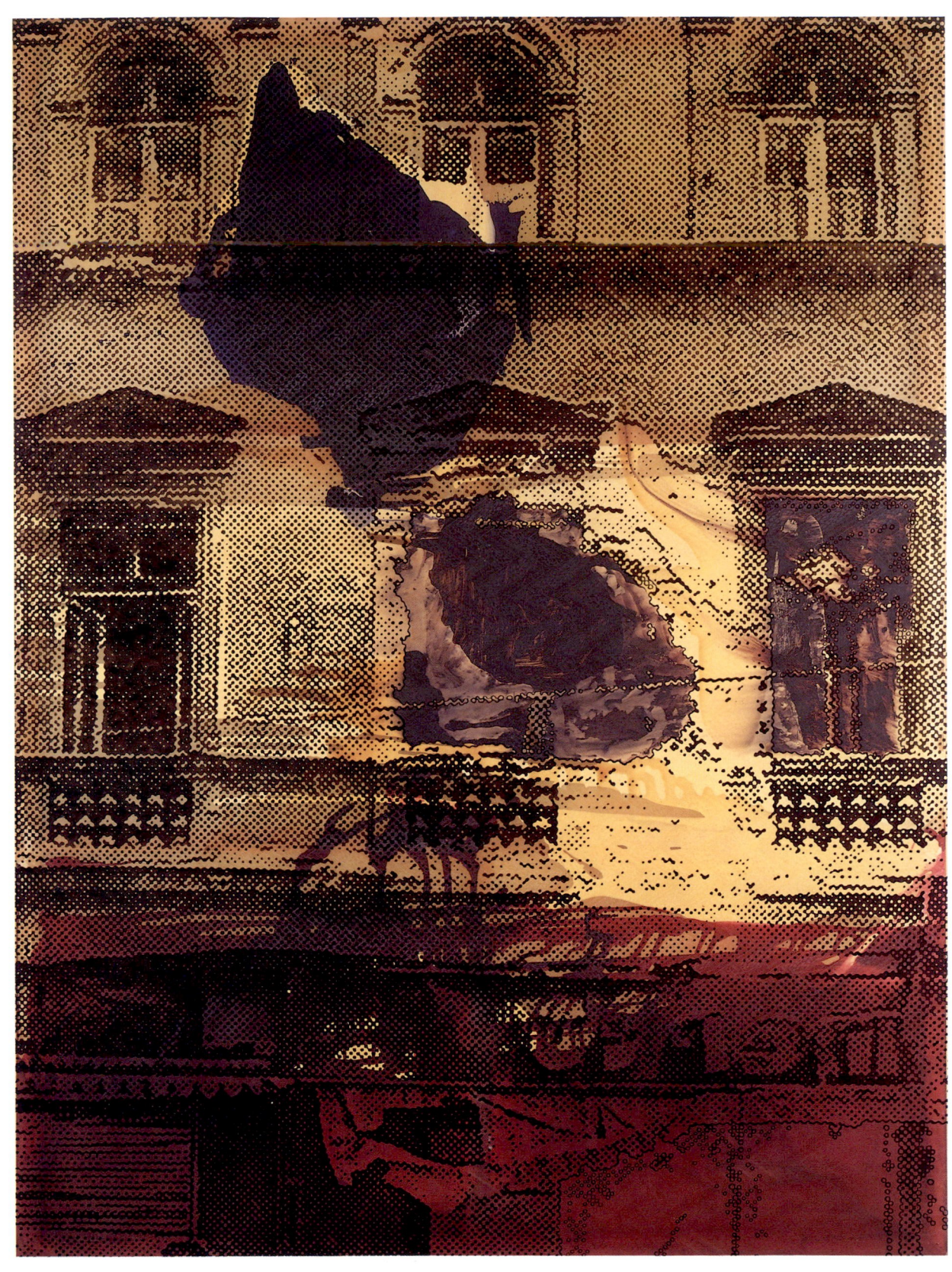

56. *Ruin* 1994

100

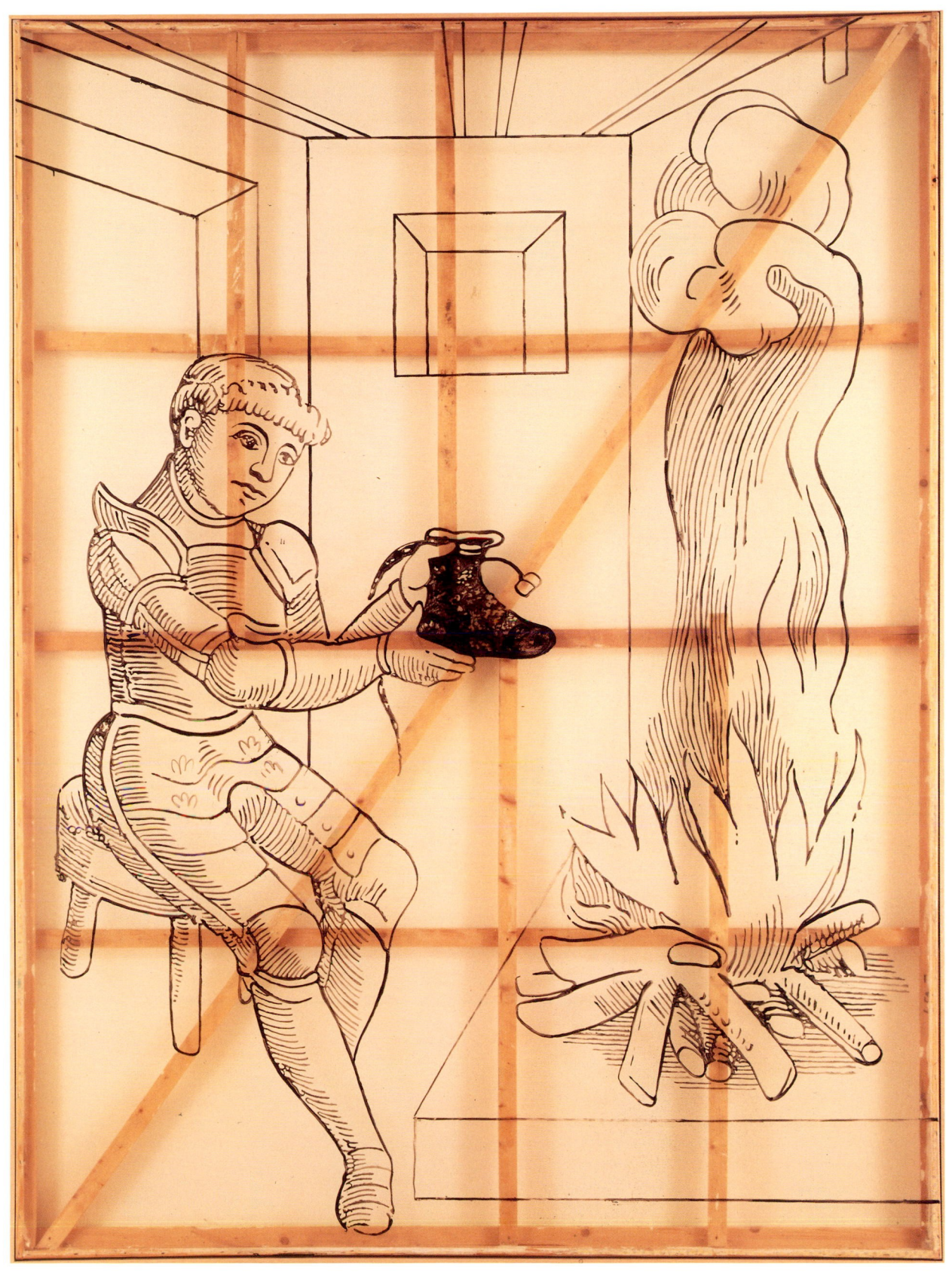

62. *Knight* 1994

List of Works

Dimensions in millimetres:
height × width × depth

1
Wardrobe 1963
lacquer on canvas
497 × 582
Private Collection
(p 27)

2
Two Palm Trees 1964
artificial resin on fabric
900 × 750
Private Collection
(p 11)

3
Sausages 1964
oil on canvas
492 × 578
Collection Froehlich, Stuttgart
(p 28)

4
5 Dots Painting 1964
dispersion on fabric
900 × 750
Collection Froehlich, Stuttgart
(p 32)

5
Buttons 1965
acrylic on canvas
1000 × 1200
Collection Froehlich, Stuttgart
(p 31)

6
The Duke and Duchess of Windsor
1965
acrylic on canvas
350 × 425
Helen van der Meij
(p 30)

7
Berliner 1965
acrylic on canvas
1600 × 1250
Collection Garnatz
(p 29)

8
Vase I 1965
acrylic on canvas
1000 × 900
Collection Garnatz
(p 35)

9
Arch 1965
oil on fabric
1800 × 1500
Private Collection
(p 33)

10
Girlfriends 1965
oil on canvas
1500 × 1900
Collection Froehlich, Stuttgart
(p 13)

11
Snowdrops 1965
dispersion and silver poster
paint on plywood
720 × 720
Collection Froehlich, Stuttgart
(p 34)

12
Woman at the Mirror 1966
acrylic on fabric
1250 × 800
Private Collection, London
(p 17)

13
Nude with Squares 1966
oil on canvas
800 × 600
Collection Froehlich, Stuttgart
(p 37)

14
Untitled Head 1966-8
latex, dispersion on canvas
1150 × 992
Private Collection
(p 38)

15
Potato House 1967
Painted wooden construction,
potatoes
2400 × 2000 × 2000
Block Collection, Denmark
(p 46)

16
Solutions V 1967
lacquer on burlap
1500 × 1250
Collection Speck, Cologne
(p 41)

17
Carl Andre in Delft 1968
dispersion on fabric
880 × 750
Collection Speck, Cologne
(p 36)

18
Modern Art 1968
acrylic, lacquer on canvas
1500 × 1250
Block Collection, Denmark
(p 39)

19
White Obelisk 1968
artificial resin on fabric
1050 × 900
Private Collection, Cologne
(p 42)

20
Polke's Whip 1968
photographs, rope, wood and tape
590 × 700
IVAM. Instituto Valenciano de
Arte Moderno - Generalitat,
Valenciana
(p 40)

21
Heron Painting II 1968
dispersion on flannel
1900 × 1500
Private Collection, Courtesy
Thomas Ammann Fine Art,
Zürich
(p 8)

22
Profile 1968
acrylic on fabric
900 × 700
Collection Froehlich, Stuttgart
(p 14)

23
The Higher Powers Command:
Paint the Right Hand Corner
Black 1969
lacquer on canvas
1500 × 1255
Collection Froehlich, Stuttgart
(p 43)

24
Alice in Wonderland 1971
mixed media on fabric strips
3200 × 2600
Raschdorf Collection,
Düsseldorf
(p 45)

25
Table Turning 1981
dispersion on fabric
1800 × 2200
Collection Speck, Cologne
(p 57)

26
Paganini 1981-3
dispersion on fabric
2230 × 5040
Private Collection, Courtesy
Thomas Ammann Fine Art,
Zürich
(p 18)

27
Scissors 1982
acrylic and ferrous mica on
canvas
2900 × 2900
Raschdorf Collection,
Düsseldorf
(p 63)

28
Magnetic Landscape 1982
acrylic and ferrous mica on
canvas
2900 × 2900
Raschdorf Collection,
Düsseldorf
(p 62)

29
Landscape 1982
artificial resin and mixed media
on canvas
1800 × 1500
Raschdorf Collection,
Düsseldorf
(p 68)

30
Black Man 1982
artificial resin, alcohol diluted
pigment, beeswax on canvas
1800 × 1500
Raschdorf Collection,
Düsseldorf
(p 69)

31
Negative Value I: Alkor 1982
oil, pigment of violets and red
lead underpainting on canvas
2600 × 2000
Raschdorf Collection,
Düsseldorf
(p 58)

32
Negative Value II: Mizar 1982
oil, pigment of violets and red
lead underpainting on canvas
2600 × 2000
Raschdorf Collection,
Düsseldorf
(p 59)

33
Negative Value III: Aldebaran
1982
oil and pigment of violets on
canvas
2600 × 2000
Raschdorf Collection,
Düsseldorf
(p 60)

34
Violet (Goya) 1982
mixed media on canvas
1500 × 1800
Private Collection
(not illustrated)

35
Colossus 1982
mixed media on canvas
1500 × 1800
Private Collection
(not illustrated)

36
Comet 1982
mixed media on canvas
1500 × 1800
Private Collection
(p 88)

37
Ghost 1982
mixed media on canvas
1500 × 1800
Private Collection
(p 83)

38
White Man 1982
mixed media on canvas
1800 × 1500
Private Collection
(not illustrated)

39
*This is how you sit correctly (after
Goya)* 1982
acrylic on fabric
2000 × 1900
Private Collection, Baden-
Baden
(p 67)

40
*Hannibal with his Armoured
Elephants* 1982
lacquer on canvas
2600 × 2000
Collection Froehlich, Stuttgart
(p 20)

41
Wig 1983
acrylic on fabric
2900 × 2900
Raschdorf Collection,
Düsseldorf
(p 65)

42
Madam Tucher's Veil 1983
artificial resin and acrylic on
canvas
2600 × 2000
Private Collection
(p 87)

43
Georg and Gugu 1983
acrylic on fabric
2200 × 4600
Georg Polke
(p 70)

44
Lapland Journey I 1994
2000 × 1600
mixed media
Private Collection
(p 72)

45
Lapland Journey II 1994
2000 × 1600
mixed media
Private Collection
(p 73)

46
*Lapland Journey III (Adoration of
the Kings: before Leonardo)* 1984
2000 × 1600
mixed media
Private Collection
(p 74)

47
*Lapland Journey IV (Adoration of
the Kings: after Leonardo)* 1984
2000 × 1600
mixed media
Private Collection
(p 75)

48
Lapland Journey V (Leonardo)
1984
2000 × 1600
mixed media
Private Collection
(p 76)

49
Untitled (Spots) 1986
pigment, lacquer, resin on
canvas
2600 × 2000
Private Collection
(p 66)

50
Swimming Pool 1988
lacquer on synthetic cotton
2550 × 3000
Collection Froehlich, Stuttgart
(p 79)

51
Childrens Games (Jeux d'enfants)
1988
artificial resin and acrylic on
fabric
2200 × 3000
MNAM, Centres Georges
Pompidou, Paris
Gift of the Société des amis du
MNAM, 1989
(p 85)

52
Annunciation 1992
artificial resin, lacquer on fabric
2250 × 3000
Private Collection
(p 97)

53
Tea Towels 1994
fabric on canvas
3000 × 2250
Private Collection
(p 24)

54
Roccoco 1994
mixed media on canvas
2900 × 2900
Private Collection
(p 95)

55
Lapis Lazuli I 1994
pigment, binder on canvas
2250 × 3000
Private Collection
(p 96)

56
Ruin 1994
artificial resin, lacquer on fabric
4000 × 3000
Private Collection
(p 100)

57
The Three Lies of Painting 1994
artificial resin, lacquer on fabric
3000 × 4000
Private Collection
(p 99)

58
Jeep 1994
artificial resin, lacquer on fabric
2250 × 3000
Private Collection
(p 80)

59
Refugee Camp 1994
artificial resin, lacquer on fabric
3000 × 5000
Private Collection
(p 92)

60
Shrapnel 1994
mixed media on canvas
1800 × 1500
Private Collection
(p 91)

61
Blue Boucher 1994
mixed media on canvas
1900 × 2000
Private Collection
(p 94)

62
Knight 1994
artificial resin, lacquer on fabric
3000 × 2250
Private Collection
(p 101)

63
Measuring Clothes 1994
fabric and paint on canvas
2300 × 3000
Private Collection
(p 23)

Biography

1941
Born 13 February in Oels, Silesia (now Olesnica, Poland)

1953
Emigrated to West Germany

1959
Studied glass painting in Düsseldorf-Kaiserwerth

1961–7
Studied at the Kunstakademie (Art Academy), Düsseldorf, under Karl Otto Goetz and Gerhard Hoehme

1963
First public exhibition, Düsseldorf

1966
German Youth Art Prize (with Klaus Geldmacher and Dieter Krieg)
First one-person shows, Berlin and Düsseldorf

1970–1
Lecturer at Hochschule für bildende Künste (Academy of Fine Arts), Hamburg

1975
Painting Prize, *XIII Bienal de São Paulo*
Professor at the Hochschule für bildende Künste (Academy of Fine Arts), Hamburg

1982
Will Grohmann Prize, Berlin

1984
Kurt Schwitters Prize, Hanover

1986
Golden Lion Prize for painting, *XLII Venice Bienale*

1987
Lichtwark Prize, Hamburg

1990
International Prize for Painting, State of Baden-Württemberg

1991
Professor at Ecole des Beaux-Arts, Hamburg

1994
Erasmus Prize, Amsterdam

Solo Exhibitions

* denotes exhibition catalogue

1966
Galerie h, Hanover (with Gerhard Richter)*
Sigmar Polke, Galerie René Block, Berlin*
Hommage à Schmela, Galerie Schmela, Düsseldorf

1967
Sigmar Polke: Neue Bilder, Galerie Heiner Friedrich, Munich

1968
Galerie René Block, Berlin, and *Kunstmarkt*, Cologne

1969
Galerie René Block, Berlin
Galerie Rudolf Zwirner, Cologne

1970
Galerie Heiner Friedrich, Munich (with Chris Kohlhöfer)
Sigmar Polke, Galerie Konrad Fischer, Düsseldorf
Kabinett für aktuelle Kunst, Bremerhaven
Bilder und Zeichnungen, Galerie Toni Gerber, Bern
Galerie Thomas Borgmann, Cologne
Galerie Michael Werner, Cologne

1971
Galerie Ernst, Hanover
Galerie Konrad Fischer, Düsseldorf

1972
Galerie Rochus Kowallek, Frankfurt
Galerie Michael Werner, Cologne
Zeichnungen, Galerie Graphikmeyer, Karlsruhe
Galerie im Goethe-Institut, Provisorium, Amsterdam
Der Dürer-Hase und Anderes Arbeiten, 1964–1972, Galerie Toni Gerber, Bern

1973
Galerie Konrad Fischer, Düsseldorf
Franz Liszt kommt gern zu mir zum Fernsehen (with Achim Duchow), Westfälisches Kunstverein, Münster*
Sigmar Polke: Bilder, Galerie Michael Werner, Cologne
Galerie Loehr, Frankfurt

1974
Original & Falschung (with Achim Duchow), Städtisches Kunstmuseum, Bonn*
Galerie Loehr, Frankfurt
Hallo Shiva, Galerie Toni Gerber/Bea Hegnauer, Zürich
Sigmar Polke, Galerie Klein, Bonn*
Galerie Cornels, Baden-Baden
Sigmar Polke: Bilder, Galerie Michael Werner and Thomas Borgmann in the Galerie Rudolf Zwirner, Cologne

1975
Galerie Klein, Bonn
Mu Nieltman Netorruprup (with Achim Duchow), Kunsthalle and Schleswig-Holsteinischer Kunstverein, Kiel
Galerie Michael Werner, Cologne

Day by Day They Take Some Brain Away (with Georg Baselitz and Blinky Palermo), *XIII Bienal de São Paulo**

1976
Bilder, Tücher, Objekte: Werkauswahl, 1962–1971, Kunsthalle, Tübingen. Travelled to Städtische Kunsthalle, Düsseldorf; and Stedelijk Van Abbemuseum, Eindhoven*
Seriaal, Helen van der Meij, Amsterdam
Wir Kleinbürger: Zeitgenossinnen und Zeitgenossen, Galerie Toni Gerber, Bern

1977
Sigmar Polke: Fotos/Achim Duchow: Projektionen, Kunstverein, Kassel*
Galerie Klein, Bonn

1978
Galerie Centro, Oldenburg
Sigmar Polke: Fotos, Galerie Gerhild Grolitsch, Munich
Sigmar Polke, InK, Halle für internationale neue Kunst, Zürich*
Sigmar Polke, Galerie Hetzler & Keller, Stuttgart

1979
Galerie Bama, Paris
Galerie Klein, Bonn

1980
Galerie Klein, Bonn
Galerie Rudolf Zwirner, Cologne

1981
Sie fliegen wieder, Galerie Toni Gerber, Bern

1982
Sigmar Polke, Galerie Bama, Paris
Sigmar Polke: Works, 1972–1981, Holly Solomon Gallery, New York

1983
Oldenburger Kunstverein, Oldenburg
Zeichnungen, 1963–1968, Galerie Michael Werner, Cologne*
Skizzenbuch aus der Jahre 1968–1969, Städtisches Museum Abteiberg, Mönchengladbach*
Sigmar Polke: Carte... Foto... Tele, Studio d'Arte Cannaviello, Milan
Sigmar Polke: Paris, Febr–März 71, Serie 39 Fotounikate, Galerie Thomas Borgmann, Cologne
Sigmar Polke: Retrospektive, Galerie Toni Gerber, Bern
Sigmar Polke, Museum Boymans-van Beuningen, Rotterdam Travelled to Städtisches Kunstmuseum, Bonn, 1984*

1984
Galerie Klein, Bonn
Galerie Nächst St Stephan, Vienna
Sigmar Polke, Kunsthaus, Zürich. Travelled to Josef-Haubrich Kunsthalle, Cologne*
Sigmar Polke: Paintings, Marian Goodman Gallery, New York

1985
Mary Boone/Michael Werner Gallery, New York
Sigmar Polke, Galerie Bama, Paris
Sigmar Polke: Recent Paintings, Antony d'Offay Gallery, London
Alfred Kren Gallery, New York*
Galerie Schmela, Düsseldorf
Sigmar Polke: Neue Bilder, Galerie Toni Gerber, Bern

1986
Sigmar Polke, Mary Boone/Michael Werner Gallery, New York
Sigmar Polke: Bilder, Thomas Borgmann-Kunsthandel, Cologne
Sigmar Polke: Frabproben – Material Versuche – Probierbilder aus den Jahren 1973–1986, Galerie Klein, Bonn
Athanor, XLII Venice Bienale*
Sigmar Polke: Titel gibt's nicht, Galerie Schmela, Düsseldorf
Sigmar Polke: Neue Bilder, Kunsthalle, Hamburg
Sigmar Polke: Offsets, Galerie Gabriele von Loeper, Hamburg
Sigmar Polke: Biennale Venedig 1986, Städtisches Museum Abteibert, Mönchengladbach*
Sigmar Polke: Fotografie, Galerie Gugu Ernesto, Cologne

1987
Sigmar Polke: Drawings from the 1960s, David Nolan Gallery, New York*
Sigmar Polke: Arbeiten auf Papier, Galerie Ha Jo Müller, Cologne

1988
Sigmar Polke: Zeichnungen, Aquarelle, Skizzenbücher, 1962–1988, Städtisches Kunstmuseum, Bonn*
Sigmar Polke, Musée d'Art Moderne de la Ville de Paris/ARC*, Paris
Sigmar Polke/Andy Warhol: From the Martin and Geertjan Visser Collections, Museum Boymans-van Beuningen, Rotterdam
Sigmar Polke: Drawings, 1963–1969, Mary Boone/Michael Werner Gallery, New York
Sigmar Polke: Peintures récentes, Galerie Crousel-Robelin/Bama, Paris

1989
Sigmar Polke: Photographien, Paris 1971, Jablonka Galerie, Cologne*
Sigmar Polke, Mary Boone Gallery, New York*
Carl Andre, Sigmar Polke, Kunstforum, Munich*

1990
Sigmar Polke: Fotografien, Staatliche Kunsthalle, Baden-Baden*
Sigmar Polke: Arbeiten auf Papier, Galerie Marie-Louise Werth, Hochfelden CH
Sigmar Polke: Peintures récentes, Galerie Crousel-Robelin/ Bama, Paris
Die Graphik des Kapitalistischen Realisus, Daniel Buchholz, Cologne
Sigmar Polke, San Francisco Museum of Modern Art, San Francisco*. Toured to Hirshhorn Museum and Sculpture Garden, Smithsonian Institution, Washington DC; Museum of Contemporary Art, Chicago; The Brooklyn Museum, New York.

1991
Sigmar Polke: Sfumato, Museo di Capodimonte, Naples*

1992
Sigmar Polke, Stedelijk Museum, Amsterdam*
Sigmar Polke: Neue Bilder, Städtisches Museum,
Mönchengladbach*

1993
Sigmar Polke: Bilder, Galerie Klein, Bonn
Sigmar Polke, Fundació Espai Poblenou, Barcelona

1994
Sigmar Polke, Portikus, Frankfurt
Sigmar Polke, Carré d'art, Musée d'Art Contemporain, Nimes*
Sigmar Polke, IVAM, Centro Julio Gonzales, Valencia*

1995
Sigmar Polke: Join the Dots, Tate Gallery Liverpool, Liverpool*

Selected Group Exhibitions

1963
Demonstrative Ausstellung in Düsseldorf, Kaiserstrasse, (with Manfred Kuttner, Konrad Lueg, and Gerhard Richter), Düsseldorf

1964
Neodada Pop Decollage Kapitalistischer Realismus, Galerie René Block, Berlin
Neue Realisten, Galerie Parnass, Wuppertal

1965
Lueg, Polke, Richter, Galerie Orez, The Hague
Galerie Heiner Friedrich, Munich (with Joseph Beuys and Cy Twombly)
Galerie h, Hanover
Galerie PRO, Bad Godesburg
Hommage à Berlin, Galerie René Block, Berlin*
Phänomene und Realitäten, Galerie René Block bei Rowohlt - Verlag, Reinbeck bei Hamburg*
Tendenzen, Städtisches Museum, Trier*

1966
Deutscher Künstlerbund 14. Ausstellung, Essen*
Düsseldorfer Künstler, Kunstverein, Wolfsburg
Extra, Städtisches Museum, Wiesbaden*
Junge Generation: Maler und Bilder in Deutschland, Akademie der Künste, Berlin*
Kunstpreis der deutschen Jugend, Staatliche Kunsthalle, Baden-Baden
Das Nichtbarocke in der Kunst, Galerie René Block, Berlin

1967
Artypo, Stedelijk Van Abbemuseum, Eindhoven*
Kunstmarkt, Cologne*
Demonstrative 1967, Galerie Heiner Friedrich, Munich
Hommage à Lidice, Galerie René Block, Berlin. Travelled in 1968 to Caput Galerie, Hamburg: Galerie Spala, Prague*
Neuer Realismus, Haus am Waldsee, Berlin. Travelled to Kunstverein, Brunswick*
Figurationen, Württembergischer Kunstverein, Stuttgart*
Wege '67, Museum am Ostwall, Dortmund; Goethe-Institut, Brussels*

1969
Accrochage II, Onnasch-Galerie, Berlin
Blockade '69: Räume von Beuys, Palermo, Hödicke, Panamarenko, Lohaus, Giese, Knoebel, Ruthenbeck, Polke, Galerie René Block, Berlin*
Kunstmarkt, Cologne*
Düsseldorfer Szene, Kunstmuseum, Lucerne*
Industrie und Technik in der deutschen Malerei, Wilhelm Lehmbruck Museum, Duisberg*
Konzeption-Conception: Dokumentation einer heutigen Kunstrichtung, Städtisches Museum Schloss Morsbroich, Leverkusen*
Neue Landschaften, Galerie von Loeper, Hamburg*
Sammlung Helmut Klinker, Städtisches Museum, Bochum*

1970

Jetzt: Kunst in Deutschland heute, Kunsthalle, Cologne*
Malerei nach Fotografie: Von der Camera Obscura bis zur Pop Art, Münchener Stadtmuseum, Munich*
New Multiple Art, Whitechapel Art Gallery, London*
Objects, Philadelphia Museum of Art, Philadelphia*
Pop-Sammlung Beck, Rheinisches Landesmuseum, Bonn*
Strategy: Get Arts, Richard Demarco Gallery, Edinburgh International Festival*
Zeichnungen I, Städtisches Museum Schloss Morsbroich, Leverkusen*. Travelled to Kunsthaus, Hamburg; Kunstverein, Munich
Zeitgenossen, Kunsthalle, Recklinghausen*

1971

20 Deutsche, Onnasch-Galerie, Berlin, and Cologne*
Düsseldorf: Stadt der Künstler, Kulturamt der Stadt Düsseldorf*
Entwürfe, Partituren, Projekte: Zeichnungen, Galerie René Block, Berlin*
Kunst Markt, Cologne*
Fünf Sammler, Kunst unserer Zeit, Von der Heydt-Museum, Wuppertal*
Multiples: The First Decade, Philadelphia Museum of Art*, Philadelphia
Polke, Palermo, Richter, Galerie Annemarie Verna, Zürich
Prospect 71, Projection, Städtische Kunsthalle, Düsseldorf; Louisiana Museum, Humlebaek, Denmark*

1972

Amsterdam Paris Düsseldorf, Solomon R Guggenheim Museum, New York*
Kunst Markt, Cologne*
Documenta 5, Kassel*
Zeichnungen 2, Städtisches Museum Schloss Morsbroich, Leverkusen*
Zeichnungen der deutschen Avantgarde, Galerie im Taxis-palais, Innsbruck*

1973

Aspekte der gegenwärtigen Kunst in Nordrhein-Westfalen, Städtisches Kunsthalle, Recklinghausen*
Between 7, Städtische Kunsthalle, Düsseldorf*. Travelled to Gallery House, Goethe-Institut, London, under title *Some 260 Miles from here: Art from the Rhein-Ruhr Germany, 1973*
Bilder, Objekte, Filme, Konzepte: Sammlung Herbig, Städtische Galerie im Lenbachhaus, Munich*
Deutsche Zeichnungen der Gegenwart, Kunsthalle, Bielefeld* Travelled to Kunstverein, Oslo; Griffelkunst, Hamburg; Kulturgeschichtliches Museum, Osnabrück
Kunst aus Fotografie: Was machen Künstler heute mit Fotografie?, Kunstverein, Hanover*
Medium Fotografie: Fotoarbeiten bildender Künstler von 1910 bis 1973, Städtisches Museum Schloss Morsbroich, Leverkusen. Travelled in 1974 to Kunstverein, Hamburg; Haus am Waldsee, Berlin; Westfälischer Kunstverein, Münster*
Prospect '73: Maler/Painters/Peintres, Städtische Kunsthall, Düsseldorf*

1974

Demonstrative Fotografie, Kunstverein, Heidelberg*
First Exhibition, René Block Gallery, New York
Internationale Kunstmesse, Basel*
Kunst bleibt Kunst: Projekt '74, Aspekte internationaler Kunst am Anfang der 70er Jahre, Wallraf-Richartz Museum and Kunsthalle, Cologne*
Multiples: Ein Versuch die Entwicklung des Auflagenobjektes darzustellen/An Attempt to Present the Development of the Object-Edition, Neuer Berliner Kunstverein, Berlin*
Neue Editionen, Galerie Edition Staeck, Heidelberg*
Surrealität-Bildrealität, 1924–1974: In den unzähligen Bildern des Lebens, Städtische Kunsthalle, Düsseldorf. Travelled to Staatliche Kunsthalle, Baden-Baden, 1975*

1975

Galerie Bama, Paris
Internationale Kunstmesse, Basel*
Tenth Exhibition, René Block Gallery, New York*

1977

Documenta 6: Handzeichnungen. Utopisches Design, Bücher, Documenta, Kassel*
Pejling af Tysk Kunst: 21 kunstnere fra Tyskland, Louisiana Museum, Humlebaek, Denmark*

1978

Works from the Crex Collection, Zurich/Werke aus der Sammlung Crex, Zürich, InK, Halle für internationale neue Kunst, Zürich. Travelled to Louisiana Museum, Humlebaek, Denmark; Städtische Galerie im Lenbachhaus, Munich; Stedelijk Van Abbemuseum, Eindhoven*
Internationale Kunstmesse, Basel*
The Book of the Art of Artists' Books, Teheran Museum of Contemporary Art*

1979

Für Jochen Hiltmann: Eine Solidaritäts, Hochschule für bildende Künste, Hamburg*
Fünf in Köln: Buthe, Polke, Rosenbach, Rühm, Schuler, Kunstverein, Cologne*
Schlaglichter: Ein Bestandsaufnahme aktueller Kunst im Rheinland, Rheinisches Landesmuseum, Bonn*
Zeichen setzen durch Zeichnen, Kunstverein, Hamburg*
With a Certain Smile, InK, Halle für internationale neue Kunst, Zürich*
30 Jahre Kunst in der Bundesrepublik Deutschland: Die Sammlung des Städtischen Kunstmuseums Bonn, Städtisches Kunstmuseum, Bonn*

1980

Art in the Seventies, Venice Bienale*
De la photographie: 17 artistes allemands, Goethe-Institut, Paris*
Treffpunkt Parnass Wuppertal, 1945–1965, Von der Heydt Museum, Wuppertal*
Vorstellungen und Wirklichkeit, 7 Aspekte subjektiver Fotografie, Städtisches Museum Schloss Morsbroich, Leverkusen. Travelled to Künstlerhaus, Vienna; Palais des Beaux-Arts, Brussels*

1981

Art allemagne aujourd'hui: Différents Aspects de l'art actuel en République Féderale d'Allemagne, Musée d'Art Moderne de la Ville de Paris/ARC, Paris*

Les Genevois collectionnent aspects de l'art d'aujourd'hui, Musée Rath and Musée d'Art et d'Histoire, Geneva*

Avantgarden-Retrospektiv: Kunst nach 1945, Westfälischer Kunstverein, Münster*

Highligts: Rückblick Oppenheim Studio Köln 1973–1979, Städtisches Kunstmuseum, Bonn*

A New Spirit in Painting, Royal Academy of Art, London*

Westkunst: Zeitgenössische Kunst seit 1939, Rheinhallen, Cologne*

1982

Avanguardia, Transavanguardia, Mura Aurealiane, Rome*

Choix pour aujourd'hui, Centre Georges Pompidou, Paris*

Crossroads Parnass: International Avant-Garde at Galerie Parnass, Wuppertal, 1949–1965, Goethe-Institut, London. Travelled to Goethe-Institut, Paris; Musées de la Ville de Bourges*

Documenta 7, Kassel*

German Drawings of the 60s, Yale University Art Gallery, New Haven; Art Gallery of Ontario, Toronto*

Kunst nu/Kunst unserer Zeit, Groninger Museum, Groningen, Netherlands*

Kunstmuseum Düsseldorf, 20 Jahrhundert: Gemälde, Skulpturen, Objekte, Städtische Kunsthalle, Düsseldorf*

Medium Fotografie 8: Künstler arbeiten mit Fotos, Kunsthalle, Kiel*

'Nieuwe' Schilderkunst, Akademie voor Beeldende Kunsten, Arnhem, Netherlands*

Sammlung Ulbricht, Städtisches Kunstmuseum, Bonn. Travelled to Neue Galerie am Landesmuseum Joanneum, Graz; Kunstmuseum, Düsseldorf*

Vergangenheit, Gegenwart, Zukunft: Zeitgenössische Kunst und Architektur, Württembergischer Kunstverein, Stuttgart*

Werke aus der Sammlung Crex/Works from the Crex Collection, Kunsthalle, Basel*

Zeitgeist, Martin-Gropius-Bau, Berlin*

Bilder und Zeichnungen, Galerie Gugu Ernesto, Cologne

1983

Kunst mit Photographie: Die Sammlung Dr. Rolf H. Krauss, Nationalgalerie, Berlin; Kunstverein, Cologne; in 1984 to Stadtmuseum, Munich; Kunsthalle, Kiel; Schleswig-Holsteinischer Kunstverein, Stuttgart*

Kunst nach 45 aus Frankfurter Privatbesitz, Kunstverein, Steinernes Haus am Römerburg, Frankfurt*

New Art at the Tate Gallery, 1983, Tate Gallery, London*

To the Happy Few: Bücher, Bilder, Objekte aus der Sammlung Reiner Speck, Kunstmuseen, Krefeld*

Works on Paper, Anthony d'Offay Gallery, London

Michael Buthe: Briefe/Sigmar Polke: Zeichnungen, Galerie Toni Gerber, Bern

Zeichnung, Gouache, Collage, Galerie Gugu Ernesto, Cologne

Zeichnungen, Arbeiten auf Papier, Kunstverein, Oldenburg*

Paintings, Installations, Stedelijk Van Abbemuseum, Eindhoven

Photo, Reihen, Galerie Elke Dröscher, Frankfurt

Kosmische Bilder in der Kunst des 20. Jahrhunderts, Staatliche Kunsthalle, Baden-Baden*

1984

Aspekte der Schönheit in der zeitgenössischen Kunst, Städtische Kunsthalle, Düsseldorf*

Aufbrüche: Manifeste, Manifestationen, Städtische Kunsthalle, Düsseldorf*

Drawings, Mary Boone/Michael Werner Gallery, New York

La Grande Parade: Hoogtepunten van de schilderkunst na 1940/Highlights in Painting after 1940, Stedelijk Museum, Amsterdam*

An International Survey of Recent Painting and Sculpture, Museum of Modern Art, New York*

Little Arena: Drawings and Sculptures from the Collection of Adri, Martin, and Geertjan Visser, Rijksmuseum Kröller-Müller, Otterlo*

ROSC '84: The Poetry of Vision, Dublin*

Medium Fotografie, Galerie Gugu Ernesto, Cologne

Treppen: 30 Künster zu einem Thema, Galerie Gugu Ernesto, Cologne

Umgang mit der Aura: Lichtbild, Abbild, Sinnbild, Städtische Galerie, Regensberg*

Von hier aus: 2 Monate neue deutsche Kunst in Düsseldorf, Messegelände Halle, Düsseldorf*

Contemporary Perspectives 1984, Center Gallery, Bucknell University, Lewisburg, Pennsylvania; Sordoni Art Gallery, Wilkes College, Wilkes-Barre, Pennsylvania*

1985

Alles und noch viel mehr: Das poetische ABC, die Katalog Anthologie der 80er Jahre, Kunsthalle and Kunstmuseum, Bern*

Arbeiten auf Papier, Galerie Loehrl, Mönchengladbach

Carnegie International, Museum of Art, Carnegie Institute, Pittsburgh*

Deutsche Kunst seit 1960: Aus der Sammlung Prinz Franz von Bayern, Staatsgalerie moderner Kunst, Munich*

The European Iceberg: Creativity in Germany and Italy Today, Art Gallery of Ontario, Toronto*

Nouvelle Biennale de Paris, 1985, Grande Halle de la Villette, Paris*

Genommen Kurven: 20 Jahre Edition Staeck, Kunstmuseum, Düsseldorf*

German Art in the Twentieth Century: Painting and Sculpture, 1905–1985, Royal Academy of Art, London*. Travelled to Staatsgalerie, Stuttgart in 1986.

Måleriska Resor, Galerie Leger, Malmö, Sweden

Rheingold: 40 Künstler aus Köln und Düsseldorf/40 Artisti da Colonia e Düsseldorf, Palazzo della Società Promotrice delle Belle Arti, Turin*

100 Jahre Kunst in Deutschland, 1885–1985, Weiterbildungszentrum, Ingelheim am Rhein*

1945–1985: Kunst in der Bundesrepublik Deutschland, Nationalgalerie, Berlin*

Vom Zeichnung, Aspekte der Zeichnung, 1960–1985, Kunstverein, Frankfurt*

Zeichner in Düsseldorf, 1955–1985, Kunstmuseum, Düsseldorf*

Medium Photographie, Kunstverein, Oldenburg

Zeichnungen aus Köln, Edition Hundertmark, Cologne

Zoographie: Tiere in der zeitgenössischen Kunst, Galerie Gmyrek, Düsseldorf*

1986

Accrochage: Baselitz, Beuys, Höckelmann, Penck, Polke, Richter, Thomas Borgmann-Kunsthandel, Cologne

Das Automobil in der Kunst, 1886–1986, Haus der Kunst, Munich*

Tableaux abstraits, Centre national d'art contemporaine, Villa Arson, Nice*

Europa/Amerika: Die Geschichte einer künstlerischen Faszination seit 1940, Museum Ludwig, Cologne*

Falls the Shadow, Recent British and European Art: 1986 Hayward Annual, Hayward Gallery, London*

Beuys zu ehren, Städtische Galerie im Lenbachhaus, Munich*

Kunst als Kultur = Art as Culture: Recent Art from Germany, Wesleyan University, Middletown, Connecticut*

Ooghoogte/Eye Level: Stedelijk Van Abbemuseum, 1936–1986, Stedelijk Van Abbemuseum, Eindhoven*

Origins, Originality, and Beyond: The Sixth Biennale of Sydney, The Biennale, Sydney*

Positionen: Malerei aus der Bundesrepublik Deutschland, Neue Berliner Galerie; Albertinum, Dresden*

Prospect '86: Eine internationale Ausstellung aktueller Kunst, Kunstverein and Schirin Kunsthalle, Frankfurt*

Die Sammlung Toni Gerber im Kunstmuseum Bern, Kunstmuseum, Bern*

Die 60er Jahre: Köln, Weg zur Kunstmetropole, vom Happening zum Kunstmarkt, Kunstverein, Cologne*

The Spiritual in Art: Abstract Painting, 1890–1985, Los Angeles County Museum of Art. Travelled in 1987 to Museum of Contemporary Art, Chicago; Haags Gemeentemuseum, The Hague*

Wild, Visionary, Spiritual: New German Art, Art Gallery of South Australia, Adelaide. Travelled to Art Gallery of Western Australia, Perth; National Art Gallery, Wellington*

Anthony d'Offay Gallery, London

Dietmar Werle, Cologne

Galerie Gabriele von Loeper, Hamburg

Focus on the Image: Selections from the Rivendell Collection, Phoenix Art Museum. Travelled in 1987–1990 to six venues in North America*

1987

Accrochage, Galerie Michael Werner, Cologne

Avant-Garde in the Eighties, Los Angeles County Museum of Art, Los Angeles*

Brennpunkt Düsseldorf, 1962–1987, Kunstmuseum, Düsseldorf*

L'Epoque, la mode, la morale, la passion: Aspects de l'art d'aujourd'hui, 1977–1987, MNAM, Centre Georges Pompidou, Paris*

Exotische Welten, Europäische Phantasien, Württembergischer Kunstverein, Stuttgart*

Galerie Neuendorf, Frankfurt*

Implosion: Eet Postmodernt Perpektiv/A Postmodern Perspective, Moderna Museet, Stockholm*

Künstlichkeit und Wirklichkeit, Volkshochschule, Wuppertal*

Multiples, Galerie Daniel Buchholz, Cologne

Warhol/Beuys/Polke, Milwaukee Art Museum; Contemporary Arts Museum, Houston*

Menschenbild aus der Maschine, Galerie Sonne, Berlin

Tableaux abstraits, Centre nationale d'art contemporain, Villa Arson, Nice*

Perspectives cavaliéres, Ecole régionale supérieure d'expression plastique, Tourcoing, France*

Waldungen: Die Deutschen und ihr Wald, Akademie der Künste, Berlin*

Watercolors by Joseph Beuys, Blinky Palermo, Sigmar Polke, Gerhard Richter, Goethe-Institut, London*

Works on Paper, Anthony d'Offay Gallery, London

Zauber der Medusa: Europäische Manierismen, Wiener Künstlerhaus, Vienna*

1988

Arbeit in Geschichte, Geschichte in Arbeit, Kunsthaus and Kunstverein, Hamburg*

Carnegie International, Carnegie Museum of Art, Pittsburgh*

Punt de confluència: Joseph Beuys, Düsseldorf, 1962–1987, Centre National de la Fundació Caixa de Pensions, Barcelona*

Joseph Beuys, Sigmar Polke, Cy Twombly, Hirschl & Adler Modern, New York*

Köln sammelt: Zeitgenössische Kunst aus Kölner Privatbesitz, Museum Ludwig, Cologne*

Das Licht von der anderen Seite: Teil II Fotografie, Monika Sprüth Galerie, Cologne

Made in Cologne, DuMont Kunsthalle, Cologne*

Mythos Europa: Europa und der Stier im Zeitalter der industriellen Zivilisation, Kunsthalle, Bremen; Wissenschaftszentrum, Bonn*

The Saatchi Collection, Saatchi Gallery, London

Refigured Painting: The German Image, 1960–1988, Toledo Museum of Art; travelled in 1989 to Solomon R Guggenheim Museum, New York; Williams College Museum of Art, Williamstown, Mass.; Kunstmuseum, Düsseldorf; Schirn Kunsthalle, Frankfurt*

Zeichenkunst der Gegenwart: Sammlung Prinz Franz von Bayern, Staatliche Graphische Sammlung, Neue Pinakothek, Munich*

Zeichnungen und Gouachen, Ernesto & Krips Galerie, Cologne

Graphik & Arbeiten auf Papier, Galerie Duden, Neckartailfingen, Germany

Ansichten, Westfälischer Kunstverein, Münster*

Collage-Decollage, Galerie Silvia Menzel, Berlin

1989

The Alien View, Galerie Kammer, Hamburg

Art from Köln, Tate Gallery Liverpool, Liverpool*

Bilderstreit: Widerspruch, Einheit, und Fragment in der Kunst seit 1960, Museum Ludwig, Cologne*

Blickpunkte I, Musée d'art contemporaine, Montreal*

Cragg, Gerz, Messager, Nordman, Polke, Galerie Crousel-Robelin/Bama, Paris

D & S Ausstellung, Kunstverein, Hamburg*

Departures: Photography, 1924–1989, Hirschl & Adler Modern, New York*

150 Jahre Kölnischer Kunstverein: Kölner Künstler, Kölner Galerien, Kunstverein, Cologne*

Das Foto als autonomes Bild: Experimentelle Gestaltung, 1839–1989, Kunsthalle, Bielefeld

Uber Unterwanderung/On Subversion, Galerie Sophia Ungers, Cologne

Magiciens de la terre, MNAM, Centre Georges Pompidou, Paris*

Das Medium der Fotografie ist berechtigt, Denkanstösse zu geben: Sammlung F.C. Gundlach, Kunstverein, Hamburg*

Modern Masters, Konsthall, Helsinki
Journeys, 1970–1989, Galerie Crousel-Robelin/Bama, Paris
Open Mind (Gesloten Circuits, Circuiti Chiusi), Museum van Hedendaagse Kunst, Ghent*
Peinture – Cinéma – Peinture, Centre de la Vieille Charité, Marseilles*
Photo-Kunst: Arbeiten aus 150 Jahren, Staatsgalerie, Stuttgart*
Photographs by Painters and Sculptors: Another Focus, Karsten Schubert, London
Repetition, Hirschl & Adler Modern, New York*
Von Dürer bis Baselitz: Deutsche Zeichnungen aus dem Kupferstichkabinett der Hamburger Kunsthalle, Kunsthalle, Hamburg*
Yves Klein, Brice Marden, Sigmar Polke, Hirschl & Adler Modern, New York*
A Group Show, Marian Goodman Gallery, New York
Farbe rot, Galerie Sylvia Menzel, Berlin
Exchange, Germany-Ireland, Goethe Institut, Dublin
Portrait, Galerie Ascan Crone, Hamburg
Robert Bechtle, Chuck Close, Robert Cottingham, Malcolm Morteg, Sigmar Polke, Pat Hearn Gallery, New York
Current European Trends, Evelyn Aimis Gallery, Toronto
Skulls, Galerie Susanne Ottesen, Copenhagen
Drawing as itself, The National Museum of Art, Osaka

1990
The Fifth Essence, Gracie Mansion Gallery, New York
Affinities and Intuitions: The Gerald S. Elliott Collection of Contemporary Art, The Art Institute of Chicago*
Die Graphik des Kapitalistischen Realismus, Daniel Buchholz, Cologne
Kombination: Klaus Gaida, Sigmar Polke, Lothar Römer, Stephan Runge, Galerie Ha Jo Müller, Cologne
Energieen/Energies, Stedelijk Museum, Amsterdam
Pharmakon '90, Makuhari Messe, Nippon Convention Center, Chiba
Blau – Farbe der Ferne, Heidelberger Kunstverein, Heidelberg
Contemporary German Photography, David Nolan Gallery, New York
Abstrakte Kunst, Wolfgang Wittrock Kunsthandel, Düsseldorf
Camera Works – Fischl, Richter, Polke, Kippenberger, Traquandi, Bustamante, Boltanski, Dokoupil, Baumgarten, Galerie Samia Saouma, Paris

1991
The Fugitive Image: Georg Herold, Jiri Georg, Dokoupil, Andy Warhol, Sigmar Polke, Perry Rubenstein, New York
German Prints; Baselitz, Polke, Richter, Susan Sheehan Gallery, New York
Nature – Création du Peintre/Natur – Schöpfung des Malers, Musée Cantonal des Beaux-Arts, Lausanne
L'art moral, Galerie Nothelfer, Berlin
Bildlicht, Museum Moderner Kunst im Museum des 20 Jahrhunderts, Vienna
This land ..., Marian Goodman Gallery, New York
Accrochage, Galerie Rudolf Zwirner, Köln
Miquel Barcelo, Georg Baselitz, Anselm Kiefer, Per Kirkeby, Sigmar Polke, Robert Rauschenberg, Andy Warhol, Galerie Faurschou, Copenhagen

Zuericher Kuenstler Was Nun, Museum Baviera, Zürich

1992
Arbeiten auf Papier, Galerie Fahnemann, Berlin
Abstrakte Malerei zwischen-Analyse und Synthese, Galerie Nächst St Stephan, Vienna
To start a Collection, Galerie Wanda Reiff, Amsterdam
Le Portrait dans l'Art Contemporain, Musée d'Art Moderne et d'Art Contemporain, Nice
Lagerfeuer, Galerie Hubert Winter, Vienna
Words don't come Easy, Kunsthaus Hamburg, Hamburg
Gotthard Graubner, Sigmar Polke, Gerhard Richter, Gemälde, Aquarelle, Graphiken, Galerie Schönewald und Beuse, Krefeld
Kabinett, Gemälde Grafik, Galerie Hübner & Thiel, Dresden
Photography in Contemporary German Art, Dallas Museum of Art, Dallas; Guggenheim Museum, Soho, New York*
Allegories of Modernism, The Museum of Modern Art, New York*

1993
European & American Drawings 1961–1969, Nolan/Edkman Gallery, New York
... sogar der Fachmann staunt!, Wolfgang Wittrock, Düsseldorf
Deutschsein?, Städtische Kunsthalle, Düsseldorf
Azur, Fondation Cartier, Jouy-en-Josas
XLV Venice Bienale, Venice
Photographie in der Deutschen Gegenwartskunst, Museum Ludwig, Cologne
Die Sprache moderner Bilder – Deutsche Kunst nach 1945, Galerie Landesgirokasse in Zusammenarbeit mit der Galerie Neher, Essen

1993–1994
Stadt & Land, Galerie Joachim Blüher, Cologne
Lovis-Corinth-Preis 1993: Ausstellung der Preisträger, Museum Ostdeutsche Galerie, Regensburg
Kunst aus Wintermärchen-Deutschland, Tochigi Prefectural Museum of Fine Arts, Tochigi, Japan

1994
Stadt und Land, Gesellschafd für Gegenwartskunst Augsburg, Holbeinhauss, Augsburg
Painting, Drawings & Sculpture, Anthony d'Offay Gallery, London
NICAF – Nippon International Contemporary Art Fair, Yokohama, Japan
Deutsche Kunst 1964–1994, Festspielbezirk, Salzburger Festspiele, Salzburg

Selected Bibliography

For a full bibliography, see *Sigmar Polke*, San Francisco Museum of Modern Art, 1990.

Monographs

Block, R, *Grafik des Kapitalistischen Realismus (Brehmer, Hödicke, Lueg, Polke, Richter, Vostell)*, Stolpe Verlag, Berlin, 1967.

Block, R, *Grafik des Kapitalistischen Realismus... bis 1971*, Edition René Block, Berlin, 1971.

Block, R, *K P Brehmer, K H Hödicke, Sigmar Polke, Gerhard Richter, Wolf Vostell, Werkzeichnisse der Druckgrafik september 1971 bis mai 1976*, Edition René Block, Berlin, 1976.

Vogel, C-Freitag, E, 'S P Verzeichnis der Druckgrafik 1966-1974' in *Mu Netorruprup*, Kunsthalle Kiel, Kiel, 1975.

Gachnang, J, *Polke-Zeichnungen 1963-1969*, Hg Verlag Gachnang & Springer, Berna-Berlin, 1987.

Parkett, no 30, 1991, texts by Bice Curiger, G Rodger Denson, Gary Garrells, Lazlo Glozer, Dave Hickey, Thomas McEvilley.

Schulz-Hoffman, C-Bischoff, U, *Sigmar Polke: Schleifenbilder*, Edition Cantz, Stuttgart, 1992.

Solo exhibition catalogues

Sigmar Polke, 'Franz Liszt kommt gern zu mir Fernsehen', texts by Jean-Christophe Ammann, Fritz Heubach, Klaus Honnef, Westfälischer Kunstverein, Münster, 1973.

Sigmar Polke, 'Original + Fälschung', text by Dierk Stemmler, Städtisches Kunstmuseum, Bonn, 1974.

Sigmar Polke, 'Nu Nieltnam Netorruprup', text by Jens Christian Jensen, Kunsthalle and Kunstverein, Kiel, 1975.

Sigmar Polke, 'Day by day they take some brain away', text by Evelyn Weiss, introduction by Kathrin Steffen, XIII Bienal de São Paulo, 1975.

Sigmar Polke: Bilder – Tücher – Objekte, Werauswahl 1962-1972, text by Sigmar Polke, Kunsthalle Tübingen; Kunsthalle Düsseldorf; Stedelijk van Abbemuseum Eindhoven; Cologne, 1976.

Sigmar Polke: fotos; Achim Duchow: Projektionen, text by Peter Breslaw, Kunstverein, Kassel, 1977.

Sigmar Polke, text by Sabine Kimpel, Städtisches Museum Mönchengladbach, 1983.

Sigmar Polke, texts by Wim Beeren, Dierk Stemmler, Hagen Lieberknecht, Sigmar Polke, Museum Boymans van Beuningen, Rotterdam, 1983; Städtisches Kunstmuseum, Bonn, 1984.

Sigmar Polke, texts by Harald Szeemann, Dietrich Helms, Siegfried Gohr, Sigmar Polke, Kunsthaus, Zürich, 1984.

Sigmar Polke 'Athanor', text by Dierk Stemmler, XLII Venice Bienale, 1986.

Sigmar Polke: Drawings from the 1960s, text by Prudence Carlson, David Nolan Gallery, New York, 1987.

Sigmar Polke: Zeichnungen, Aquarelle, Skizzenbücher 1962-1988, texts by Katharina Schmidt, Gunter Schweikhart, Kunstmuseum, Bonn, 1988.

Sigmar Polke, texts by Suzanne Pagé, Bernard Marcadé, Bice Curiger, Michael Oppitz, Hagen Lieberknecht, Feelman & Dietman, Musée d'Art Moderne de la Ville de Paris, ARC, Paris, 1988.

Sigmar Polke: Fotografien, texts by Jochen Poetter, Bice Curiger, Kunsthalle, Baden-Baden, 1990.

Sigmar Polke, texts by John Caldwell, Peter Schjeldahl, John Baldessari, Reiner Speck, San Francisco Museum of Modern Art, San Francisco, 1990.

Sigmar Polke, texts by Wim Beeren, Peter Sloterdijk, Bice Curiger, Ursula Pia Jauch, Stedelijk Museum, Amsterdam, 1992.

Sigmar Polke: Neue Bilder, text by Dierk Stemmler, Städtisches Museum Mönchengladbach, 1992.

Sigmar Polke, texts by Guy Tosatto, Bernard Marcadé, Carré d'Art, Musée d'Art Contemporain, Nimes, 1994.

Sigmar Polke, texts by Guy Tosatto, Bernard Marcadé, Kevin Power, IVAM Centre del Carme, Valencia, 1994.

Sigmar Polke: Join the dots, texts by Sean Rainbird, Judith Nesbitt, Thomas McEvilley, Tate Gallery Liverpool, Liverpool, 1994.

This book is published to accompany an exhibition organised by
Tate Gallery Liverpool
Sigmar Polke: Join the Dots
21 January – 17 April 1995

Prepared by Tate Gallery Liverpool
Published and distributed by Tate Gallery Publications,
Millbank, London SW1P 4RG

Edited by Judith Nesbitt

Designed by Herman Lelie
Typeset by Goodfellow & Egan Ltd, Cambridge
Printed by Balding + Mansell, Peterborough

Vignettes are taken from Franz Pocci, *Lustiges Komödienbüchlein*, vols I and II,
Leipzig, 1907 and *Lustige Rasperlkomödien*, Leipzig, 1925. Franz Pocci
(1807–1876) was an author and illustrator of children's books, and a musician.

Photographic credits:

p 22 reproduced courtesy Stedelijk Museum, Amsterdam
p 46, 49 reproduced courtesy of Michael Werner Gallery,
Cologne and New York
p 50 reproduced courtesy Private Collection, London
p 51 © Dr Reiner Speck, Cologne
pp 72–6 © Fridtjof Varsnel, Amsterdam

All Sigmar Polke works © Sigmar Polke

Front cover: *Knight* 1994
Back cover: *Polke's Whip* 1968
Frontispiece: Photograph by Wolfgang Wesener

Distributed by Tate Gallery Publications, London
ISBN 1-85437-1533

Distributed in Germany, Austria and Switzerland by Oktagon Verlag, Stuttgart
ISBN 3-927789-87-9

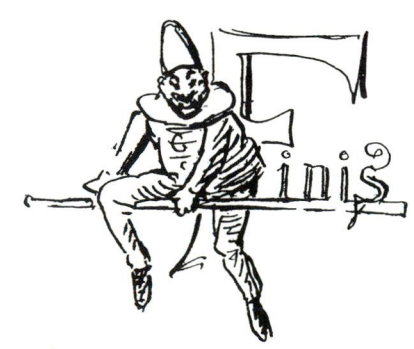